Race, Gender and the Black Feminist Theory

Beginning from the premise that psychology needs to be questioned, dismantled and new perspectives brought to the table in order to produce alternative solutions, this book takes an unusual transdisciplinary step into the activism of Black feminist theory. The author, Suryia Nayak, presents a close reading of Audre Lorde and other related scholars to demonstrate how the activism of Black feminist theory is concerned with subjects central to radical critical thinking and practice, such as identity, alienation, trauma, loss, the position and constitution of individuals within relationships, the family, community and society.

Nayak reveals how Black feminist theory seeks to address issues that are also a core concern of critical psychology, including individualism, essentialism and normalization. Her work grapples with several questions at the heart of key contemporary debates concerning methodology, identity, difference, race and gender. Using a powerful line of argument, the book weaves these themes together to show how the activism of Black feminist theory in general, and the work of Audre Lorde in particular, can be used to effect social change in response to the damaging psychological impact of oppressive social constructions.

Race, Gender and the Activism of Black Feminist Theory will be of great interest to advanced students, researchers, political activists and practitioners in psychology, counselling, psychotherapy, mental health, social work and community development.

Suryia Nayak is a senior lecturer in social work at the University of Salford, UK. She has 30 years' experience of working in the Rape Crisis Movement, community engagement across a diverse range of peoples positioned as alienated using models of education as liberation, and the activism of Black feminism to raise consciousness about the psychological and political impact of oppressive social constructions.

Concepts for critical psychology: disciplinary boundaries re-thought
Series editor: Ian Parker

Developments inside psychology that question the history of the discipline and the way it functions in society have led many psychologists to look outside the discipline for new ideas. This series draws on cutting edge critiques from just outside psychology in order to complement and question critical arguments emerging inside. The authors provide new perspectives on subjectivity from disciplinary debates and cultural phenomena adjacent to traditional studies of the individual.

The books in the series are useful for advanced level undergraduate and postgraduate students, researchers and lecturers in psychology and other related disciplines such as cultural studies, geography, literary theory, philosophy, psychotherapy, social work and sociology.

Published Titles:

Surviving Identity
Vulnerability and the psychology of recognition
Kenneth McLaughlin

Psychologisation in Times of Globalisation
Jan De Vos

Social Identity in Question
Construction, subjectivity and critique
Parisa Dashtipour

Cultural Ecstasies
Drugs, gender and the social imaginary
Ilana Mountian

Decolonizing Global Mental Health
The psychiatrization of the majority world
China Mills

Race, Gender and the Activism of Black Feminist Theory

Working with Audre Lorde

Suryia Nayak

Routledge
Taylor & Francis Group

LONDON AND NEW YORK

First published 2015
by Routledge
27 Church Road, Hove, East Sussex BN3 2FA

and by Routledge
711 Third Avenue, New York, NY 10017

Routledge is an imprint of the Taylor & Francis Group, an informa business

British Library Cataloguing in Publication Data
A catalogue record for this book is available from the British Library

Library of Congress Cataloging-in-Publication Data
Nayak, Suryia.
Race, gender, and the activism of Black feminist theory : working with
Audre Lorde / Suryia Nayak.
pages cm. – (Concepts for critical psychology)
Includes bibliographical references and index.
1. Womanism–United States. 2. Feminist theory–United States.
3. Feminism–United States. 4. African American women. I. Title.
HQ1197.N39 2014
305.420973–dc23
2014005065

ISBN: 978-1-84872-174-6 (hbk)
ISBN: 978-1-84872-175-3 (pbk)
ISBN: 978-0-203-52196-0 (ebk)

Typeset in Times
by Cenveo Publisher Services

I dedicate this book to my daughters, Sophia, Misha and India.

Contents

Foreword

Do you know who Audre Lorde was? When you have finished reading this book you will not only know what an extraordinarily interesting theorist and activist she was, you will also begin to grasp the consequences of her absence from the curriculum of most academic subjects. With even more signal importance for those of us who like to think we are radicals in the discipline, you will ask why it has taken so long for 'critical' researchers to admit her to their own reading lists. Suryia Nayak's strategic recovery of the work of Audre Lorde has a double purpose in this book, and she pursues the argument through a series of conceptual debates that are intimately linked with the experience and practice of those who have been and are historically and currently oppressed by dominant forms of knowledge. On the one hand there is the question of this particular individual herself, the writings of a Black feminist, and her contribution to the renewal of theory, including of critique in psychology. Through careful detailed reading of these writings and of the way they anticipate many later arguments about the nature of the intersection of 'gender', 'race', power and resistance, we are able to appreciate not only what Audre Lorde said but what her absence from psychology (for example) so far means.

There is also another deeper aim here, which is taken forward in chapters that examine the implications of those writings for social change, political activism, feminism and intersectionality. Audre Lorde exemplifies a standpoint that has been repeatedly marginalized and silenced not only in mainstream debate but also in ostensibly progressive critique. We need to reflect on the concepts we mobilize to develop a 'critical psychology' or a critical approach to subjectivity generally that connects with social change. This book shows us how important that is, and gives arguments and resources from a diverse tradition of political activism – that of Black feminism – that asks in many different ways why it is that the voices of the oppressed are not heard. We come to see that this complex, beautifully written book is not only telling us something that we should already have thought about ourselves (if this 'we' is the white masculine voice of the discipline that psychologists of whatever 'race' and 'gender' learn to speak when they train and think is a necessary expression of the identity that is awarded to them by their registration bodies) but why we did not think about it, or, if we did think about it, we quickly forgot it again.

It is not only psychology that pretends that the only good theory is psychological theory; 'critical' social theory and then the various forms of 'critical psychology' each pride themselves on having a theory that will serve to question and challenge dominant knowledge and practice. In this book, *Race, Gender and the Activism of Black Feminist Theory: Working with Audre Lorde*, the argument is deeper and far more wide-ranging than that. It becomes clear that it will not be enough to simply take on board some of the ideas of this particular Black feminist writer, the focus of this book named in the title, and absorb them into the existing corpus of already well-worked 'critical' writing. This book is 'outwith' psychology, at the boundaries not only of psychology and other disciplines but at the boundaries of 'critical psychology' and post-colonial 'critical theory'. It shows us that these Black feminist arguments are already densely elaborated theories, and deeply bound up with practice. The book moves from theory to practice and back to theory again to illuminate and warrant practice for us. White psychology will not function if the theoretical practice traced in this book is taken seriously. In its place the activism of Black feminist theory will find its place, its voice and the possibilities of social change.

Ian Parker
University of Leicester

Preface

Early in January 2013, while I was at home in the middle of the day writing this book, I was subjected to an armed burglary. The experience resonates with themes that preoccupy this re-reading of Audre Lorde, specifically with regards to: the timing, place and impact of 'epistemic violence' (Spivak, 1988: 280) visited on Black feminisms; the theft of thinking; and the disregard for, and appropriation of, the temporal and spatial dimensions of historical and socio-economic contexts that constitute Black women's lives. Armed with weapons of authenticity, historical amnesia, hierarchies of oppression, the 'always already' (Althusser, 1971) and categories of identity designed to suppress Black feminism, the violations of Black women are unannounced and uninvited. My starting point is that '[t]he shadow obscuring this complex Black women's intellectual tradition is neither accidental nor benign' (Collins, 2000: 3). This book picks up on the idea of the impossibility of hospitality (Derrida, 2000) and the 'critic as host' (Hillis Miller, 1979) to frame a critical analysis of the occupation and location of Black feminist praxis. This book negotiates 'a channel between the "high theoretical" and the "suspicious of all theories"' (Boyce Davies, 1994: 43).

The challenge of re-reading Audre Lorde is to maintain a persistent, hypervigilant sensitivity towards the hostility of 'epistemic violence' (Spivak, 1988: 280). I think it is possible to re-read Spivak's (1988) question, 'Can the Subaltern Speak?' in terms of, 'Can Black feminist theory speak?' The question of what is read and utilized and what is not, particularly when the 'what is not' refers to Black feminist scholarship in general, and to the work of Lorde in particular, is fundamental to this book.

This book produces new re-readings of Lorde's work that go beyond a literary textual analysis. The Kristevan idea of intertextuality as intersubjectivity (Kristeva, 1969: 37) is used to show that the predicaments of positionality reiterated throughout this book mirror the predicaments within the activism of all theories of liberation. This book explores questions such as: how can feminist theory present authoritative, metanarrative claims (and they need to be authoritative in the face of a racist, homophobic patriarchy that denies the legitimacy of Black women) whilst being implicated?

The quandary is that of how to establish and communicate any sense of a comprehensible, coherent re-reading of Lorde when each re-reading destabilizes and contests any notion of an 'established'. The quandary takes on particular significance in relation to Black feminist political writings and communication of political imperatives. In other words, is there a possibility of 'the transformation of silence into language and action' (Lorde, 1977: 40) in the condition of the impossibility of language? Re-reading Lorde is both to occupy the margin and to make use of the margin so that the impossible, the unavailable and the fissures of re-reading Black feminist theoretical communications are the conditions of the activism of Black feminist theory.

Three principles of Black feminist methodology that underpin the work of this book include:

• Lorde's Black feminist 'uses of the erotic' (Lorde, 1978);
• the dialogical and dialectical relationship between experience, practice and scholarship (Collins, 2000: 30);
• that methodology is contingent upon, and constituted through, Black feminist activism. Throughout this book, I make a concerted effort to transfer the text of Black feminist critical theory from the page to the day-to-day struggles of Black feminist activism. For example, I demonstrate the relevance of Lorde in terms of constructing Black-women-only reflective spaces and service provision, interventions to confront sexual violence against Black women and the 'psychological toll' (The Combahee River Collective, 1977: 266) of 'learn[ing] to lie down with the different parts of ourselves' (Abod, 1987: 158). This book is a work of re-membering; it is a deliberate transgression of fixed, theoretical and disciplinary borders, which reinvigorates the activism of theory.

Acknowledgements

I would like to thank Professor Erica Burman and Dr. Daniela Caselli for enabling me to move beyond genuflection. The intellectual integrity, rigour, care and commitment that Erica and Daniela gave to me created an experience of the activism of Black feminist theory as an exchange of knowledge, experience and creation of ideas that will stay with me always.

I would like to say a very special thank you to my beloved brother, Krisna Nayak, for his fast (in every sense of the word) intelligence, for staying alongside me in my journeys and our shared encounters of Saraswati. In particular, my gratitude goes to Krisna for never giving up on the impossibility of hospitality with me.

My gratitude goes to 'Eagle Eyes' Ru for her gentle, persistent thoroughness in helping me to proofread this book.

My gratitude goes to Mudar Patherya and his family in Kolkata for giving place to 'the absolute, unknown, anonymous other'.

I would like to acknowledge the determined courage of women survivors of sexual violence and the privilege of working with feminist activists that are core to my living.

Finally, my deepest appreciation goes to Audre Lorde, and to the network of friends and comrades who sustain me on a daily basis.

1 Introduction

Race, gender and social change

This book invites readers to re-think disciplinary boundaries by orientating critical psychology to the activism of Black feminist theory and, in particular, to ask critical psychologists to consider the work of Audre Lorde. Lorde never identified herself as a critical psychologist, but she did identify herself as a 'sister outsider' who critically examined the notion of being an outsider positioned outside of that represented as legitimate. Lorde was concerned with the ways in which Black women's psychology is constituted by and through the social contexts they inhabit. Lorde's critical social theory of 'outsider' positions makes her an ideal candidate outside of critical psychology to participate in the critique of the psy-complex,[1] and questions the borders that constitute contemporary critiques. In what could be described as one of the most detailed evaluations of Lorde's contribution to Black feminist thought, Rudolph Byrd states that: 'Lorde made ... a new critical social theory that provides us with the grammar and vocabulary to describe and define difference and the complex nature of oppression' (Byrd, 2009: 21).

There are times in this book when there is very little mention of the term 'critical psychology', and this is a challenge to the identity and constitution of critical psychology itself. However, this re-reading of Lorde is absolutely a sustained and rigorous critical analysis of the psychologization of Black women in terms of how social structures produce Black women and what Black women produce. The focus is on the ways in which racist, homophobic, patriarchal social structures create racist, homophobic, patriarchal psychic structures (Oliver, 2001: 34). Furthermore, it is about the production and function of borders.

The activism of Black feminist theory

The term 'activism of Black feminist theory' is used throughout this book to emphasize the intersection of 'activism' with 'Black feminist theory'; that is, 'activism' or 'action' that translates into concrete, tangible outputs that produce outcomes that make a measurable difference to Black women's lives. Thus, 'Black feminist theory' is brought to life and articulated as the thinking upon which the action is contingent. The emphasis on the production and function of action is vital to any approach to forms of critical psychology that analyse the relationship between theory and outcomes. hooks and West point out that:

> Theory is inescapable because it is an indispensable weapon in struggle, and it is an indispensable weapon in struggle because it provides certain kinds of understanding, certain kinds of illumination, certain kinds of insights that are requisite if we are to act effectively.
>
> (hooks & West, 1991: 34–5)

The emphasis on the activism of Black feminist theory is because the process of surviving the daily trauma of being a Black woman in the context of a racist, homophobic patriarchy needs to be understood in the context of Black women's lives. Lorde explains that:

> ... survival isn't theoretical, we live it every day. We live it on the streets, we live it in the banks, we live it with our children.
>
> (Greene, 1989: 183)

> ... those of us who have been forged in the crucibles of difference – those of us who are poor, who are lesbians, who are Black, who are older – know that *survival is not an academic skill*.
>
> (Lorde, 1979a: 112; emphasis in original)

The work of Lorde has been instrumental in providing 'certain kinds of understanding, certain kinds of illumination, certain kinds of insights that are requisite if we are to act effectively' (hooks & West, 1991: 34–5). Lorde has been positioned as outside of the discipline of critical psychology, and this book seeks to bring the translation and relevance of her work to current emancipatory approaches to practice and experience. In other words, the absence of the activism of Black feminist theory (including the work of Lorde) in critical psychology needs to be questioned. Derek Hook makes a similar point in relation to the relative absence of post-colonial thinking in critical psychology, and the issues and questions that Hook raises are relevant to the position of the activism of Black feminist theory. Speaking of writers such as Fanon, Biko and Bhabha, Hook states:

> Each of these above sets of critical formulations provide powerful ways of thinking [about] the conjunction of the psychological and the

political, the affective and the structural, the psychical and the govern-mental. We have as such a powerfully critical combination of registers that one would take to lie at the centre of critical psychology's ostensibly critical concerns (Hayes, 1989; Hook, 2004a). Why then have such post- or anti-colonial thinkers not featured more strongly in the conceptual resources of critical social psychology? How might their work, and their characteristic concerns – racism, colonial discourse, cultural dispossession, alterity, psychical mutilation, resistance, etc. – alert us to gaps in the growing orthodoxy of critical psychology? To approach the question from another direction: what might be said to be the 'critical psychology' of these theorists, and particularly of Frantz Fanon and Steve Biko? How might their use of the register of the psychological within the political and their concerns with the cultural dynamics of colonisation alert us to the possibilities of psychology as a vocabulary of resistance? Furthermore, what does each of these critics have to tell us about the crowning problematic of the colonial and postcolonial condition, namely that of racism, a phenomena that seems as political as it does psychical in nature?

> (Hook, 2005: n.p.; refer to original source for details
> of citations within extract)

This book identifies and seeks to address the gap of the activism of Black feminist theory in the 'growing orthodoxy of critical psychology' not merely to fill the gap with something that is sorely missing, but to raise questions about the gap itself. Indeed, critical psychology should be alert to, and suspicious of, any orthodoxy (in any stage of its growth) because, otherwise, it will fall foul of the problematic doctrinal constructions and diagnostic categories that it seeks to contest (Henwood *et al.*, 1998). In another direction, the 'critical psychology' of the activism of Black feminist theory, and particularly of Lorde, uses the register of the psychological within the political that provides a language, model and practice of resistance. It could be argued that this is actually the reason for the gap; one has to wonder why such vital registers, scholarship and examples of political activism are not explicitly named at the heart of critical psychology. Sara Ahmed takes up this issue in the following way:

> I would argue that the question we need to ask is not, "should femi-nism use theory?", as feminism (as with any other political discourse) always does use theory: it is always going to involve ways of ordering the world. For me, the question is rather: "is this theoretical frame-work explicit or not?" Feminism needs to make explicit its theoretical

frameworks and it needs to do so precisely in order to re-conceptualise the relation between theory and practice.

(Ahmed, 1998: 18)

It could be argued that the constitution and impact of the teaching, debates, seminars, conferences and scholarship of critical psychology would be very different if they were built on an explicit foundation of the activism of Black feminist theory. Critical psychology would do well to remember that '[s]ocial theory in particular can serve to reproduce existing power relations or to foster social and economic justice' (Collins, 1998: xi). The tools we use, why and how we use them, what we leave out and what we include, and the connections we make between tools, reflect power relations. The point is that any hope of meaningful alliances within and outside of critical psychology to combat the psychologization of Black women will fail if Black feminist interventions, wisdom and experience continue to be marginalized. Furthermore, they will fail if any element in those alliances replicates the unequal power relations at work in the psy-complex through hegemonic thinking and positioning in those alliances, thereby replicating the very problem they seek to address.

What is critical psychology?

The structure of this book uses a re-reading of Lorde in order to examine how the activism of Black feminist theory is both effective in challenging the tactics of a racist, homophobic patriarchy and, potentially, in danger of falling foul of the very tactics it is challenging. The significance of these insights is relevant to the activism of all liberation theories, including critical psychology. Before proceeding any further, it is perhaps important to say something about what critical psychology is. Ian Parker (1999) offers four characteristics that distinguish 'critical' psychology from 'mainstream' psychology, or to put it another way, four characteristics that form the nucleus of the 'critical' and why the 'critical' goes way beyond the verb to 'criticize'. Parker's (1999: 13–15) summary is as follows:

- Critical psychology here is therefore, first of all,

  the systematic examination of how some varieties of psychological action and experience are privileged over others, how dominant accounts of 'psychology' operate ideologically and in the service of power.

(p. 13; italics in original)

• Second, then, critical psychology is,

> *the study of the ways in which all varieties of psychology are culturally historically constructed, and how alternative varieties of psychology may confirm or resist ideological assumptions in mainstream models.*
>
> (p. 13; italics in original)

• Third, then, critical psychology is,

> *the study of forms of surveillance and self-regulation in everyday life and the ways in which psychological culture operates beyond the boundaries of academic and professional practice.*
>
> (p. 14; italics in original)

• Fourth, then, critical psychology is,

> *the exploration of the way everyday 'ordinary psychology' structures academic and professional work in psychology and how everyday activities might provide the basis for resistance to contemporary disciplinary practices.*
>
> (p. 15; italics in original)

Bringing the activism of Black feminist theory to this summary of critical psychology might provoke the following questions: 'First, what does Black feminist thought confront *as* critical social theory? [...] Second, what issues does Black feminist thought raise *for* critical social theory? [...] Finally, what contributions can Black feminist thought make *to* critical social theory?' (Collins, 1998: xvii–xviii; emphasis in original). Thus, in relation to key elements highlighted by Parker's summary of critical psychology above, the activism of Black feminist theory responds to the questions raised by Collins by:

1 confronting the workings of dominant ideology assumptions in the service of power, surveillance and self-regulation;
2 raising the need to examine oppressive constructs as products of social, historical and cultural spaces;
3 contributing models of resistance to contemporary disciplinary practices.

This book takes what may, at first, seem like an unusual and surprising step across the disciplinary boundary of psychology to Lorde's political essays and speeches. Yet, the activism of Black feminist theory is concerned with issues that are central to psychology: issues such as identity, alienation, trauma, loss, the relationship between the internal and external world, and the position and constitution of the individual within relationships, the family, community and society. Furthermore, the activism of Black feminist theory tackles issues that are central to critical psychology, such as individualism, essentialism and normalization.

The psychologization of Black women

The activism of Black feminist theory questions ideological representations of the individual as separated from social relationships. Furthermore, the activism of Black feminist theory questions forms of thinking and practices that represent and diagnose social change as a form of deviance. Indeed, it could be argued that the systematic suppression of the activism of Black feminist theory, and of the women who speak and write this theory, is precisely because they are seen as a form of deviance. However, it is precisely this situation of suppression that gave birth to, and continues to sustain, the activism of Black feminist theory, and it is precisely this situation of suppression that the activism of Black feminist theory confronts. The point is that the relationship between theory and context is crucial because:

> Social theory is a body of knowledge and a set of institutional practices that actively grapple with the central questions facing a group of people in a specific political, social, and historic context. Instead of circulating exclusively as a body of decontextualized ideas among privileged intellectuals, social theory emerges from, is legitimated by, and reflects the concerns of actual groups of people in particular institutional settings. This definition creates space for all types of groups to participate in theorizing about social issues. Moreover, it suggests that differences in perspective about social issues will reflect differences in the power of those who theorize.
>
> (Collins, 1998: xii)

Race, gender and social change form the nucleus of this book. It is worth stating that the focus will be on the ways that race and gender impact on Black[2] women, and this focus is taken because the impact is disproportionately negative and destructive. Parker argues that:

> Ideas about sex and race divide people from each other, and psychological theories have played an important role in making us believe that differences between people are essential, necessary qualities of human beings that can never be changed. Psychology provides ever more sophisticated and so more effective arguments for sexism and racism

than the old biological theories, and this new psychology as ideology serves to justify violence and reinforce stereotypes.

(Parker, 2007: 2)

Race and gender are issues that illustrate how ideology and surveillance within the psy-complex (Hook *et al*., 2004; Parker, 2005; Parker & Revelli, 2008; Rose, 1998) function to create and maintain categories and criteria of 'the normal', 'the healthy' and 'the well-adjusted' individual and community. However, race and gender form the nucleus of this book for another reason; that is, as the activism of Black feminist theory teaches, dismantling the conceptual apparatus that constructs race and gender offers lessons for the dismantling of the conceptual apparatus that constructs 'psychologization'. Furthermore, the activism of Black feminist theory on race and gender offers models for radical social change.

The critical tendencies of outsiders

The activism of Black feminist theory meets the challenge required of critical psychology as outlined by Parker in the following terms:

> To arrive at even the barest elements of a definition of 'critical psychology' we need to develop a cultural-historical account of the emergence of different 'critical' tendencies, and we have to make 'critical links' between the many activities that define themselves as critical. Our conception of 'boundaries' then needs to be questioned if we are to be able to collect these tendencies and activities together; boundaries which divide those who are inside from those outside the discipline, which divide academics, professionals and users of services, and divide those who are properly and improperly critical.

(Parker, 1999: 3)

A particular 'critical' tendency of the activism of Black feminist theory is the questioning of the concept, function and production of boundaries. The activism of Black feminist theory has emerged, and continues to emerge, out of a cultural-historical context that positions, represents and constitutes Black women as outsiders. Indeed, the act of Black women giving voice to these 'critical tendencies' has been, and continues to be, used as a basis for psychological diagnoses of mental illness that serve to pathologize Black women. In other words, Black women's thinking has been characterized as 'improperly critical' and placed on the psychologically abnormal side of the boundary. Carole Boyce Davies describes the position Black women have been forced to occupy in terms of the notion of Black women as migratory subjects who occupy 'that in-between space that is neither here nor there' (Boyce Davies, 1994: 1). Lorde defines racism and sexism as: '*Racism, the belief in the inherent superiority of one race over all others and thereby the right to dominance. Sexism, the belief in the inherent superiority of one sex over the other and thereby the right to dominance*' (Lorde, 1980a: 115; italics in original). The focus on race and gender is precisely because the daily reality of living with the effects of racism and sexism, mixed up with other pressures such as poverty, disability and homophobia, is exhausting. The pernicious problem of racism is described by Lorde in the following way:

> Black women and our children know the fabric of our lives is stitched with violence and with hatred, that there is no rest ... For us, increasingly, violence weaves through the daily tissues of our living – in the supermarket, in the classroom, in the elevator, in the clinic and the schoolyard, from the plumber, the baker, the saleswoman, the bus driver, the bank teller, the waitress who does not serve us.
>
> (Lorde, 1980a: 119)

Then, to add insult to injury, '[t]here is a very low value placed upon Black women's psyches in this society, which is both racist and sexist' (The Combahee River Collective, 1977: 266).

Racism and sexism produce mental illness and so-called mental disorders. However, in order to deflect attention away from these daily experiences as inherent to social processes, they are treated by psychology as inherent to the people who experience these oppressive social processes (Parker, 2007: 4). In the context of a racist, homophobic patriarchy, Black women are constituted as the abject subject defined by Kristeva as 'what disturbs identity, system, order. What does not respect borders, positions, rules. The in-between, the ambiguous, the composite' (Kristeva, 1982: 4). It is little wonder, then, that Black women are acted upon by psychological practices so that the disturbance and lack of conformity of Black women are contained. The injustice is that Black women are positioned by social constructions as 'what disturbs identity, system, order' and then targeted by those same social constructions as requiring containment, order and boundaries. Black women are experienced and represented as excess in every sense of Bill Ashcroft's exploration of the word:

> Too much, too long, too many, too subversive, too voluble, too insistent, too loud, too strident, too much-too-much, too complex, too hybrid, too convoluted, too disrespectful, too antagonistic, too insistent, too insistent, too insistent, too repetitive, too paranoid, too ... excessive.
>
> (Ashcroft, 1994: 33; ellipsis in original)

Each identity category that constitutes the subjectivity of the Black woman is excessive in itself. The infinite referral and deferral of intersections of excess produce excess, and are felt as an excess. This excess is manufactured into a pathological disorder based on diagnostic criteria and codes that focus clinical attention on the 'too much-too-much' aspect of behaviour and thought (American Psychiatric Association, 2013). The ways in which women are excessively physically, emotionally and sexually violated, and survive these experiences of excess, need to be understood in relation to racism and those other weights of oppression that press down on Black women.

Lorde explains that '[t]here is a constant drain of energy which might be better used in redefining ourselves and devising realistic scenarios for altering the present and constructing the future' (Lorde, 1980a: 115). However, even though it would be logical to assume that Black women are in a good position to articulate, redefine and devise 'realistic scenarios for altering the present and constructing the future', this is not the case because the voices, standpoints and scholarship of Black women are often ignored and/or sidelined for not being recognized as having any efficacy. In a particularly unjust move, this situation of silencing the voice and denying the potency of Black women becomes seen as part of the inherent 'natural' characteristic and position of Black women. In other words, that which is externally imposed becomes inscribed in, and recognized as part of, the Black woman's pathology. This pathology is recognized as 'abnormal' and, as such, is a pathology that needs correcting: first, in order to highlight the fact of the abnormality, thereby creating a distinct and recognizable division between 'normal' and 'abnormal'; and second, in order to contain the abnormality and to even attempt, perhaps, to turn the 'abnormal' into something more 'normal'. The emphasis on race and gender seeks to dismantle 'how mainstream psychological theory and/or method exclude, ignore or misrepresent vast groupings of people by virtue of psychology's unquestioned allegiance to white, Indo-European males as normative' (Holzman, 2011: 3).

No apolitical scholarship

The question of what is read and utilized and what is not, particularly when the 'what is not' refers to the activism of Black feminist scholarship in general, and to the work of Lorde in particular, is fundamental to the relationship between race, gender and critical psychology. In other words, '[t]here can, of course, be no apolitical scholarship' (Mohanty, 1984: 19). This book is a decisive intervention with the deliberate intention of troubling the knowledge/power relation, recognizing that:

> ... the production of discourse is at once controlled, selected, organised and redistributed by a certain number of procedures whose role is to

ward off its powers and dangers, to gain mastery over its chance
events, to evade its ponderous, formidable materiality.

(Foucault, 1981: 52)

The 'number of procedures' that Foucault speaks of include socially
constructed ideological, diagnostic and material divisions based on concepts
and categories such as the mad, abnormal, bad and wrong. These divisions
function to rank who can and who cannot speak with any legitimacy. For
example, one of the procedures of the knowledge/power relation is to
produce those who count as theorists and those who do not count as theorists. In the cultural–historical context of a racist, homophobic patriarchy,
it is no coincidence that emancipatory approaches such as the activism of
Black feminist theory, which emerges out of, and confronts, the oppressions of racism, sexism and homophobia, are particularly incisive in
confronting 'the production of discourse' (Foucault, 1981: 52). It is for this
reason that this book places emphasis on the 'links between Black feminism as a social justice project and Black feminist thought as its intellectual
center' (Collins, 2000: xi). It is a direct challenge to the binaries of activism
or theory, and experience or scholarship. This book insists that critical
psychology engages in the activism of Black feminist theory 'as its intellectual center'.

Spivak focusses on the crux of the matter in relation to who is read, used
and heard in her question, 'Can the Subaltern Speak?' (Spivak, 1988). In
response, this book re-reads Spivak's question, 'Can the Subaltern Speak?',
in terms of 'Can the activism of Black feminist theory speak?' or, indeed,
'Can psychologized Black women speak?' Any understanding of the ways
in which power operates through the discipline and practices of the psy-
complex needs to incorporate, on the one hand, an understanding of the
ways that Black women are represented, the ideology that supports these
representations and how these constitute Black women's represented
subjectivity; and on the other hand, the political, economic and governmen-
tal contexts that produce representations. This is a shift away from the
individual as the site of analysis to the ways that individuals are produced
within the contexts that produce them. It requires an intersection of 'theory
of representation and the political economy of global capitalism' (Spivak,
1988: 271). It could be argued that 'any approach that does not pay heed to
this "relationship" cannot hope to effect sustainable change to either our
own thoughts, feelings and experiences or to the circumstances that are
implicated in their creation' (Nightingale & Cromby, 2001: 117).

My starting point is that '[t]he shadow obscuring this complex Black
women's intellectual tradition is neither accidental nor benign' (Collins,
2000: 3). This book demonstrates unequivocally that the activism of Black

feminist theory in general, and Lorde's work in particular, has relevance to legitimately intervene in, and shape the direction of, contemporary debates in critical psychology. Indeed, not to do so is both a loss and to be complicit with, to return to Spivak's statement, 'Western intellectual's role' in maintaining unequal relations of power (Spivak, 1988: 271). It demonstrates the ways in which Lorde, in conjunction with the activism of Black feminist scholarship, creates a critical lens not only to examine key concepts, issues and questions, but also to provide a body of theory relevant for applied disciplines such as critical psychology, social work, psychoanalysis, social theory, critical race theory and feminism.

Complexity of the task

The focus on race and gender is particularly complex for several interconnected reasons. Race as an identity category is both complex and unhelpful because race is not a stable, natural, biological phenomenon – it is an unstable social construction used as a mechanism to subordinate and divide certain categories of people (Back & Solomos, 2000; Banton, 1998; Cashmore & Jennings, 2001; Davis, 1981; Hall, 1997; Loring Brace, 2005; Parker & Song, 2001; Seshadri-Crooks, 2000a). Similarly, gender is not a natural, biological phenomenon – it is an unstable social construction used as a mechanism to subordinate and divide certain categories of people (Beauvoir, 2010; Butler, 2006). Kalpana Seshadri-Crooks' explanation of the function of racial signifiers contains principles that can be applied to both race and gender. She explains that:

... words like black and white, when used as nouns – works like names. That is, they are rigid designators – they are signifiers that have no signified. [...] it may be more productive to view racial color designators as operating not unlike proper names. The proper name is neither wholly one's own (i.e., we are all named by others) nor is it meaningful. [...] No set of qualitative descriptions can establish black or white identity across all possible worlds, but we cannot therefore say that black and white do not exist.

(Seshadri-Crooks, 2000a: 141; parentheses in original)

In other words, nouns such as 'Black', 'white', 'mixed race', 'man', 'woman' and 'transgender' are unable to establish any stable, fixed meaning, representation or identity category 'across all possible worlds', yet these nouns exist and act as pointers for recognition. The key is not in the noun(s), but how the nouns act as envelopes or containers that transport and transform racist and sexist social structures into racist and sexist psychic structures

(Oliver, 2001: 34). Psychology is a prime example of a social structure or mechanism that uses these nouns to transform that which is unstable, shifting and produced within particular contexts (for example, 'Black', 'white', 'woman' and 'man') into the myth of a stable, fixed category. Anthias and Yuval-Davis state that an effective analysis of race, gender and class 'requires exploring how exclusions and subordinations are linked to produce diverse outcomes with regard to the placement of collective subjects within the different major divisions that construct them' (Anthias & Yuval-Davis, 1993: 20). The point is that 'the placement', or positioning, 'collective subjects' (or Black women), 'different major divisions that construct' (or the 'psy-complex') are all unstable and shifting relative to historical, cultural and social contexts. Anthias and Yuval-Davis argue that:

> ... a historically contingent articulation of gender, ethnicity, race and class must draw on the analytical distinctions between the categories and their social effectivity and begin to theorize particular ways in which they interrelate in different contexts. This does not require that their interrelationship is always the same nor that one division or category is always prioritized. But it does require that we specify the mechanisms by which different forms of exclusion and subordination operate.
>
> (Anthias & Yuval-Davis, 1993: 99)

Black women have argued long and hard against being forced 'to settle for one easy definition, one narrow individuation of self' (Lorde, 1996: 197). The activism of Black feminist theory determinedly resists 'the mockeries of separations that have been imposed upon us' (Lorde, 1977: 43). Drawing on the Latin '*terminare*' or terminus in the root meaning of the word 'determine', the activism of Black feminist theory seeks an end or terminus to the systematic, endemic and persistent fragmentation of Black women's identity and experience. Lorde's determined defiance of the injustice of having parts of her identity and experience cancelled out or reduced to one component is a recurrent theme in her work.

Lorde is clear that the fragmentation of self-definition, experience and identity is an injustice. Lorde identifies three components of the injustice: the injustice is in being cut 'off from the energy that comes from all those different pieces' (Savren & Robinson, 1982: 82) of self; the injustice is in being subjected to 'the kind of turmoil that sucks energy away' (Savren & Robinson, 1982: 82); and the injustice is in the 'exclusion' (Evans, 1979: 72) of pieces of Black women's identity and experience. It is a prime example of the injustice of psychology that uses its particular knowledge base and practices to diagnose patients who are in pieces by subjecting them to interventions and ideological approaches that replicate the very process of fragmentation that is at the heart of the patients' presenting trauma. Furthermore, the injustice is that the social constructions that constitute the multiple identities and experiences of Black women are sites of oppression and discrimination. The task in resisting 'the mockeries of separations' (Lorde, 1977: 43) is that of asserting the specificity of Black women's position and experience as productions of the psy-complex, while not falling into the trap of the 'setting up of difference and heterogeneity against meta-prescriptions and universality ... [because to] privilege difference against totality is to keep the opposition in place' (Ahmed, 1998: 48). Furthermore, the practice of re-inscribing socially constructed borders of difference results in essentialist productions of the authentic Black woman. These inherent tensions are core to feminist debates and should be core to debates within the activism of all theories of liberation, including critical psychology. A snapshot of the kinds of issues that constitute these debates within feminism could be constructed in the form of the following imaginary conversation.[3] This invented conversation tracks the complexity of resisting the universal patriarchal subjugation of women, while attending to the specificity of women's lived experience:

AUDRE LORDE: 'Ignoring the differences of race between women and the implications of those differences presents the most serious threat to the mobilization of women's joint power. As white women ignore their built-in privilege of whiteness and define *woman* in terms of their own experience alone, then women of Color become "other", the outsider whose experience and tradition is too "alien" to comprehend' (Lorde, 1980a: 117; italics in original).

BELL HOOKS: 'Feminism has its party line and women who feel a need for a different strategy, a different foundation, often find themselves ostracized and silenced' (hooks, 1984: 9).

AUDRE LORDE: 'There is a pretense to homogeneity of experience covered by the word *sisterhood* that does not in fact exist' (Lorde, 1980a: 116).

CHANDRA TALPADE MOHANTY: 'I am trying to uncover how ethnocentric universalism is produced in certain analyses. As a matter of fact, my argument holds for any discourse that sets up its own authorial subjects as the implicit referent, that is, the yardstick by which to encode and represent cultural others. It is in this move that power is exercised in discourse' (Mohanty, 1984: 21).

ELIZABETH SPELMAN: '[P]ositing an essential "womanness" has the effect of making women inessential in a variety of ways. First of all, if there is an essential womanness that all women have and have always had, then we needn't know anything about any woman in particular. For the details of her situation and her experience are irrelevant to her being a woman. Thus if we want to understand what "being a woman" means, we needn't investigate her individual life or any other woman's individual life. All those particulars become inessential to her being and our understanding of her being a woman. And so she also becomes inessential in the sense that she is not needed in order to produce the "story of woman". If all women have the same story "as women", we don't need a chorus of voices to tell the story' (Spelman, 1988a: 236).

BELL HOOKS: 'Defined in this way, it is unlikely that women would join feminist movement simply because we are biologically the same' (hooks, 1984: 24).

SIMONE DE BEAUVOIR: 'Certainly woman like man is a human being; but such an assertion is abstract; the fact is that every concrete human being is always uniquely situated. Rejecting the notions of the eternal feminine, the black soul or the Jewish character is not to deny that there are today Jews, blacks or women: this denial is not a liberation for those concerned, but an inauthentic flight. Clearly, no woman can claim without bad faith to be situated beyond her sex' (Beauvoir, 2010: 4).

BELL HOOKS: 'As a black woman interested in feminist movement, I am often asked whether being black is more important than being a woman; whether feminist struggle to end sexist oppression is more important than the struggle to end racism and vice-versa' (hooks, 1984: 29).

KADIATU KANNEH: 'The idea that women should ignore the divisions between themselves and sweep together across class, race and national boundaries to create a post-historical Utopian home, bypasses the knowledge that racial oppression has always created the body from obsessive fantasies of biology and environment' (Kanneh, 1992: 296).

SARA SULERI: 'The claim to authenticity – only a black can speak for a black; only a postcolonial subcontinental feminist can adequately represent the lived experience of that culture – points to the great difficulty posited by the "authenticity" of female racial voices in the great game that claims to be the first narrative of what the ethnically constructed woman is deemed to want. This desire all too often takes its theoretical form in a will to subjectivity that claims a theoretical basis most clearly contravened by the process of its analysis' (Suleri, 1992: 251).

GAYATRI CHAKRAVORTY SPIVAK: 'What I find useful is the sustained and developing work on the *mechanics* of the constitution of the Other; we can use it to much greater analytic and interventionist advantage than invocations of the *authenticity* of the Other' (Spivak, 1988: 294; emphasis in original).

The dangers of using a metanarrative of liberation (in the context of this imaginary conversation, this is a metanarrative of feminism) contingent upon a 'yardstick' (Mohanty, 1984: 21) of shared identification, commonality or brand (sisterhood, critical psychology) are far reaching because:

- it undermines 'the mobilization of women's joint power' (Lorde, 1980a: 117);
- it produces and silences the '"other", the outsider whose experience and tradition is too "alien" to comprehend' (Lorde, 1980a: 117);
- it produces a situation where the details of a Black woman's 'experience are irrelevant' (Spelman, 1984a: 236) and, in such a situation of knowing, 'she is not needed in order to produce the "story of woman"' (Spelman, 1988a: 236).

These issues are relevant to how the specificity of Black women's intersectional experiences is addressed: for example, in relation to the question of Black-women-only service provision. The tension is that the very problem that gives rise to the need for Black-women-only spaces could easily become the problem that Black-women-only spaces reproduce. Here, I am imagining a Black-women-only, 'Native Informant' (Spivak, 1986: 66) 'party line' (hooks, 1984: 9) that inverts the 'inauthentic flight' (Beauvoir, 2010: 4) based on an assumed authenticity that would only reproduce essentialism.

Intersectional praxis

Even though the psy-complex is produced and functions within an intersection of issues, elements and mechanisms that legitimizes the psychologization of Black women, critical emancipatory approaches, including critical psychology, that aim to confront these oppressive intersections often fail to be interconnected. Kimberlé Crenshaw explains that:

> Although racism and sexism readily intersect in the lives of real people, they seldom do in feminist and antiracist practices. And so, when the practices expound identity as woman or person of color as an either/or proposition, they relegate the identity of women of color to a location that resists telling.
>
> (Crenshaw, 1991: 1242)

Here, Crenshaw's point is that binary positions, fragmentation and splitting that work to silence Black women's experiences become replicated within the politics and practice of challenging violence against Black women. Political, practical and policy solutions to tackle violence against women need to be founded on the interdependency of difference (Anzaldúa, 2007; Burman, 2004; Butler, 2004; Krizsan *et al.*, 2012; Lorde, 1980a; Nayak,

2013; Schiek & Lawson, 2011; Yuval-Davis, 2006, 2011). In other words, the concept and practice of interconnection is central to understanding, and working to confront, the psy-complex.

The theory of intersectionality effectively challenges mutually exclusive categories of experience and analysis. The theory of intersectionality successfully exposes that these are socially constructed borders of experience and analysis, and goes on to detail the destructive, negative consequences of separated out categories. The complexity of the task of intersectionality is articulated here by Rajagopalan Radhakrishnan:

> Each of these lived realities, such as the ethnic, the diasporic, the gay, the migrant, the subaltern, etc., must imagine its own discursive-epistemic space as a form of openness to one another's persuasion: neither totalized oppression ...
>
> (Radhakrishnan, 2000: 61)

The challenge Radhakrishnan presents here is that of understanding the particularity of lived realities that constitutes the identity and experience of Black women, whilst resisting the urge to totalize. Avtar Brah cautions that the temptation to focus on one aspect of identity or experience can lead to a situation where 'one form of oppression leads to the reinforcement of another' (Brah, 1996: 126). Rather, Brah advocates for 'strategies for challenging all oppressions on the basis of an understanding of how they interconnect and articulate' (Brah, 1996: 126). The interdependency, interconnections and intersections of multiple forms of oppression as a basis for critical psychology will only be effective if they are allowed to remain open to each other. Arguing against a unitary representation and fixed hierarchy, Homi Bhabha comments that:

> ... the transformational value of change lies in the rearticulation, or translation, of elements that are *neither the One* (unitary working class) *nor the Other* (the politics of gender) *but something else besides*, which contests the terms and territories of both.
>
> (Bhabha, 1994: 28; emphasis in original)

Critical psychology must advocate resistance to an addition and subtraction configuration of identity and experience, and invite scrutiny of 'subjugated knowledges' (Collins, 2000: 252) of 'the matrix of domination' (Hill Collins, 2000: 228). Drawing on her own experience, Lorde explains that:

> As a Black lesbian feminist comfortable with the many different ingredients of my identity, and a woman committed to racial and sexual freedom from oppression, I find I am constantly being encouraged to

pluck out some one aspect of myself and present this as the meaningful whole, eclipsing or denying the other parts of self.

(Lorde, 1980a: 120)

The mechanisms used to encourage the eclipsing of multiple aspects of Black women's identity and experience may not present as obvious or explicit. The subtle and even unwitting encouragement to pluck out one aspect of Black women's identity to formulate a stable, coherent 'whole' would be tantamount to using the '*master's tools* [to] *dismantle the master's house*' (Lorde, 1979a: 112; emphasis in original), and, as such, would fail.

Examination of Black women located within 'complex spaces of multiple meanings' (Nash, 2008: 8) is anything but neat and straightforward. Nash speaks of the need 'to grapple with intersectionality's theoretical, political, and methodological murkiness' (Nash, 2008: 1). However, the 'murkiness' is not an excuse for reductionist, satisfactory formulations that provide solutions to difficult issues. Rather, the 'murkiness' should and will remain murky. Instead of being foreclosed, this murky quality of intersectionality could be used for productive thinking that may not necessarily summon up solutions. The activism of Black feminist theory born out of intersecting subjugated knowledge in the matrix of power (Collins, 2000) offers a 'politics of location' (Boyce Davies, 1994: 153; Kaplan, 1994) that is 'pivotal to negotiating interdisciplinary, inter-subjective, psychic, emotional, political and practical solutions to the problems' (Nayak, 2013: 37) of the psycomplex. Critical analysis of 'relations of proximity [that] highlight the facts of connection or dis/connection' (Probyn, 2003: 294; see also Ahmed, 2000) is central to finding new meanings, solutions and tools.

The issue of fragmentation applies to the scholarship, conceptual frameworks and ideological approaches both within the discipline of psychology and the work of critical psychology. The principles of Norma Alarcón's critique of feminist thinking can be applied to all branches of epistemology. She states that:

> With gender as the central concept in feminist thinking, epistemology is flattened out in such a way that we lose sight of the complex and multiple ways in which the subject and object of possible experience are constituted ... There's no inquiry into the knowing subject beyond the fact of being a "woman."

(Alarcón, 1990: 361)

It could be argued that both feminism and critical psychology have a shared interest in social justice, development of emancipatory frameworks and critical analysis of oppressive constructs. If a key objective of critical psychology is to challenge the ways in which psychologization operates through the reduction of horizons in which certain issues are bracketed out, then critical psychology has to be vigilant not to operate through the reduction of horizons wrapped up in good intentions. Thus, perhaps the critique Alarcón levels at feminism could translate across to critical psychology, provoking the following questions: what are the concepts that are central to critical psychology? How do these concepts frame the epistemological lenses available to critical psychology 'in such a way that we lose sight of the complex and multiple ways in which the subject and object' (Alarcón, 1990: 361) of Black women's identity and experience are constituted? Bringing the critical lens of the activism of Black feminist theory that is positioned outside of psychology, and not explicitly present in critical psychology, may enable an 'inquiry into the knowing subject beyond' (Alarcón, 1990: 361) the limitations of that which is positioned and recognized within the epistemology of critical psychology. The activism of Lorde's Black feminist theory outlines the seductions and dangers of operating through the reduction of horizons based on an epistemology that has been flattened out in the following caution:

> And make no mistake; you will be paid well not to feel, not to scrutinize the function of your differences and their meaning, until it will be too late to feel at all. You will be paid in insularity, in poisonous creature comforts, false securities, in the spurious belief that the midnight knock will always be upon somebody else's door.
>
> (Lorde, n.d.: 204)

The arguments elaborated throughout this book are built on the foundation that a sustained focus on the intersectional experience of race and gender serves to highlight that the 'entrapments' (Lorde, 1920a: 118) used in relation to Black women have specificity in their own right that must be accounted for.

The critic as host

The text of this book could be seen as my hosting, with all of the problematics of being a host, Lorde in relation to scholars such as Bhabha, Boyce Davies, Butler, Collins, Crenshaw, Fanon, Haraway, hooks, Seshadri-Crooks and Spivak, to name but a few of the guests. This is in order to make a decisive intervention into current thinking about issues such as difference, position, voice and what Stuart Hall (1996: 17) refers to as the 'constitutive outside'. It is a deliberate transgression of fixed, theoretical and disciplinary borders to attempt a space of emotional and 'intellectual hospitality'

(Bennett, 2003 and Kaufman, 2001, cited in Molz & Gibson, 2007: 2), because 'what is at stake is not only the thinking *of* hospitality, but thinking *as* hospitality' (Friese, 2004, cited in Molz & Gibson, 2007: 2; emphasis in original). Indeed, it will become apparent that Derrida's (2000) notion of the impossibility of hospitality, in terms of who is host and who is guest, is an important methodological tool. The impossibility of hospitality is used to deconstruct the constitution, position and play of power relations with regard to the production of the 'other' and what the 'other' produces.

The psy-complex produces and uses a prolific and varied network of texts and documentation. This can be seen in the genre of (auto)biographical texts within psychology such as patient case notes, narrative therapy, life story books for adopted and looked after children, survivor testimonials and the use of diaries in psychological interventions such as Cognitive Behavioural Therapy. These texts are produced by, and exist in, a complex intertextual web (Barthes, 1967, 1971; Foucault, 1969). Furthermore, these texts function in psychology to establish authenticity, intention and notions of subjectivity and identity. Here is where, and precisely why, Black feminist scholarship and traditions of writing are a relevant critical alternative. They directly confront and destabilize bounded representations of authenticity, intention and subjectivity. Lorde grounds all of her work in her lived experience. Thus, Lorde's political essays, journals, poetry, letters, biomythography, speeches and interviews fuse the biographical and theoretical. In other words, Lorde dismantles the boundaries that are set up between the personal and the political, and, in doing so, she opens up critical alternatives for social change that build on a long and enduring Black feminist literary tradition. Pivotal to this intervention is the belief that:

> ... the question of context is not dismissed within deconstruction: it is simply held to be illimitable. That does not mean that one ought never to try to delimit a context, but only that every such attempt will be open to necessary revision.
>
> (Butler *et al.*, 2000: ix)

This book uses and insists on the use of critical close reading practices as a methodological and conceptual framework for all critical praxes. Thus, what is demonstrated is that the context of a detailed literary textual analysis of Lorde is 'illimitable'. Indeed, this book insists that the limits imposed upon Black feminist scholarship and the 'dividing practices' (Foucault, 1975, 1982) of dislocating activism from Black feminist theory must be open to 'necessary revision' (Butler *et al.*, 2000: ix). This book produces new re-readings of Lorde's work that go beyond a literary textual analysis. A prime example of this is in Kristeva's idea of intertextuality as intersubjectivity

(Kristeva, 1969: 37), which proposes that the space and place between words function as the space and place between people, ideologies, representation and subjectivities. In the context of race, gender and social change, intertextuality as intersubjectivity is invaluable as a methodological and theoretical lens to scrutinize the predicaments of positionality.

Why psychology (critical, traditional or otherwise) should read Audre Lorde

This book offers a robust case for a radical re-positioning of psychology on the foundation of the activism of Black feminist theory. This includes imagining what psychology would look like laid on a Black feminist foundation and outlining how this could be a basis for radical social change.

This book offers a critical analysis of the conceptual tools used to maintain disciplinary borders and categories of identity. Traditional qualitative and quantitative tools, methods and measures such as predictability, standardization, sampling, objectivity and repeatability are products of, and maintain, particular ideological apparatus. To prioritize questions of what a tool or method can do, and how it functions, is to miss out a vital priority question, that is, to ask: what constitutes the ideological material that the tools and methodology are cut from? Here is where psychology could learn much from the activism of Black feminist theory. The activism of Black feminist theory critically scrutinizes the methodology used to explain, measure, diagnose and cure Black women, and, in doing so, offers detailed rigorous critiques, models of dismantling components of these phenomena and alternative approaches (Gunaratham, 2003). Primarily, this book demonstrates how the subject under analysis and the tools for analysis share a structure and mode of operation that intersect, and are contingent upon each other.

The activism of Black feminist theory questions the function and production of borderlines. The clever bit about borderlines is that they create the illusion of a method to transform 'the sloppy' and 'the chaotic' into 'the neat', 'the organized' and 'the compartmentalized', while actually contributing to, and sustaining the root cause of, the problem. The dialectic is that borderlines are used to contain the very problems they produce, and the psychiatric diagnostic category of the borderline is a classic example of this. Positions on the borderline shape the subject and objects of psychology. This book uses binaries such as inside/outside, recognition/misrecognition, absence/presence, inclusion/exclusion and normal/abnormal that are usually 'taken for granted' (Burr, 1995) to illustrate the ways in which categorization, segregation and splitting function to maintain the madness and misery they purport to cure. Psychology could learn from more sophisticated models offered by Black feminist scholars such as Lorde. Black feminist models utilize the space in between constructed binaries. Lorde offers an analysis of how and why fragmentation produces psychological distress and limitations that stifle creative potential. The activism of Black feminist theory offers models that illustrate that the sum of the parts is greater than that of Western models of splitting up and dealing with parts separated out. Lorde works with the mutually constitutive relationship between intersecting parts rather than models of addition and subtraction (Crenshaw, 1989).

The discipline of psychology is constituted by what it excludes. Psychology is characterized and identified by demarcating that which belongs to it and that which does not belong to it. People become clients of psychologists because of what and where they belong, and do not belong. This process produces discourses of essentialism and authenticity, where categories of people represent, embody and perform the 'constitutive outside' (Hall, 1996: 17). The concept of 'difference' is fundamental to the logic and legitimization of the 'constitutive outside'. It is a logic that functions to mask the anxiety, ambivalence and displacement that the concept of 'difference' produces. Here is where the activism of Black feminist theory in general, and Lorde's work in particular, has much to offer in terms of deconstructing the processes and outcomes of the 'constitutive outside'. Furthermore, Lorde's work on race, gender, class, sexuality and social change outlines forms of resistance and alternative models of thinking and acting that the activism of theories of liberation ignore at their own peril.

This book uses the work of Lorde as a theoretical lens to focus on the relationship between social and psychic structures, using the examples of race and gender as mechanisms of oppression. Although progressive psychological approaches, such as psycho-social models, acknowledge the importance of context, this book uncovers the intersecting social and psychic manoeuvres in the process of subject formation. The book draws on the rich, sophisticated and often ignored work of the activism of Black feminist theory on the psychological impact of racism and sexism.

This book argues that psychology, as a discipline and practice, colonizes social and psychic spaces and relies on, and (re-)produces, mimicry (Bhabha, 1994). Mimicry is a necessary aspect of any take-over, occupation and appropriation, where X takes over Y in order to control, regulate, re-define and re-inscribe power relations. The colonization of social and psychic spaces is a key component in the role of the psy-complex and psychologization. Colonization produces anxiety and ambivalence, and psychology is an anxious colonizer. This book draws on the work of Bhabha (1994) to argue that psychology is caught up in an equation of colonization-anxiety-mimicry, controlled and masked by paranoid boundaries, where the subject and object of psychology are rigorously patrolled. Lorde articulated how colonization also involves amputation of the diseased and disordered members imported by the colonizer, and the imposition of artificial prostheses invented to camouflage, render invisible and unrecognizable, the violence performed in these processes (Lorde, 1980b). This book draws on the work of Lorde in conjunction with post-colonial Black feminist scholarship (Khanna, 2003) as a theoretical lens to scrutinize how individualism, essentialism and normalization function as tools of colonization and mimicry.

Summary of chapters

Chapter 3 argues that Lorde's (1979b: 60) statement that 'Black feminism is not white feminism in blackface' is contingent upon the fact that 'racist social structures create racist psychic structures' (Oliver, 2001: 34). This re-reading of Lorde through a re-reading of Fanon's (2008: 4) concept of 'epidermalization' goes beyond the racist regime of visibility, suggesting that the mimicry of 'blackface' includes mechanisms of the 'psychic life of power' (Butler, 1997a). Bhabha's analysis of the inevitable ambivalence of mimicry in the act of colonization is used to explore ramifications of the '*almost the same, but not quite*' (Bhabha, 1994: 86; emphasis in original) for 'Black feminism is not white feminism in blackface'.

In Chapter 4, 'The Aporetics of Intersectionality', I re-read Crenshaw's (1989) theory of intersectionality as a theory of the aporia of borders. This chapter traces the solution of unavailability in intersectionality not in order to discredit intersectionality as a solution, but rather to disrupt intersectionality as a unified solution. I argue that analytic borders created between analyses of the structural and analyses of the subject/subjective/subjectivity, using intersectionality, run counter to the spirit of intersectionality. This chapter is a reflective, theoretical investigation into the psychological turmoil of the experience of the aporia of intersectionality.

In Chapter 5, I conclude with an examination of the position and function of theory within the current context of attacks on theory. I propose a re-reading of Anzaldúa's (2007) 'La Conciencia de la Mestiza: Towards a New Consciousness' through Bion's (1959) psychoanalytic, theoretical lens of 'Attacks on Linking'. This chapter interrogates the dialectic of occupying theoretical frameworks as a site of subversion, while being mindful of Lorde's caution that '*the master's tools will never dismantle the master's house*' (Lorde, 1979a: 112; emphasis in original). In order to reiterate the relevance of the activism of Lorde's work in particular, and the activism of Black feminist theory in general, this chapter provides a number of problematics that are alive in my engagement with Black feminist, grassroots activism. Ending on Jordan's (1978) question of, 'Where Is the Love?', the conclusion points to the challenges that this book opens up in relation to a rigorous commitment to the activism of Black feminist theory.

Notes

1 The 'psy-complex' is a term used by Foucault to refer to the set of disciplines and practices concerning the psyche. These include psychology, psychiatry, psychoanalysis, psychotherapy, psychiatric nursing, psychiatric social work and criminology (Foucault, 1977; Ingleby, 1985; Parton, 1999; Rose, 1985).

2 In an interview with Pratibha Parmar and Jackie Kay that took place in London in 1988, Lorde explores the meaning of the term 'Black': 'Take the issue of how we name ourselves, for example. In the United States, Black means of African heritage and we use the term Women of Color to include Native American, Latina, Asian American women. I understand that here, Black is a political term which includes all oppressed ethnic groups, and the term Women of Color is frowned upon' (Parmar & Kay, 1988: 176). However, I acknowledge that the use of the term 'Black' is problematic and contested. Brah (1996) provides a detailed analysis of the issue, stating that: 'In practice, the category "black feminism" in Britain is only meaningful *vis-à-vis* the category "white feminism"' (Brah, 1996: 112).

I want to draw attention to problems with the term 'minority' in the frequently used term 'BME' and agree with Burman's (2005) analysis: 'We used the term "minoritization" (rather than "minority" or "minority ethnic group") to highlight that groups and communities do not occupy the position of "minority" by virtue of some inherent property (of their culture or religion, for example), but rather they come to acquire this position as the outcome of a socio-historical and political process' (Burman, 2005: 533; parentheses in original).

3 In my teaching of critical analysis, I ask students to imagine they are hosting a dinner party, bringing different voices and perspectives to the table of their analysis in conversation with each other. The imaginary conversation that structures this plays with the concepts of the speech act and speaking position that are at the core of the subject under discussion. Furthermore, it represents a performance of intertextuality in action. Drawing on a literary tradition of dialogue, conversation and interviews, as mirrored in Lorde's work, this experimental pedagogical intervention constructs an imaginary conversation between activists and scholars across a temporal and spatial spectrum that juxtaposes a range of visions, standpoints and theoretical approaches. This imaginary conversation straddles the fictional and non-fictional in the sense that the actual words of the scholars cited are juxtaposed within a fictional frame. This invented construction is a deliberate transgression of fixed, theoretical borders.

2 The political activism of close reading practices

As a method, the practice of close reading, incorporating detailed, critical deconstruction of the function and production of text, presents numerous, interrelated predicaments that are core to any critical political resistance to the psy-complex. In other words, the practice of textual analysis is not confined to the study of literature in any perceived abstract, non-applied discipline. The function and production of text are foundational to the establishment and sustainability of all State apparatus. The writing, recording and (re-)reading of documentation function to produce individuals, communities and societies. The issue is that '[k]nowledge claims are always socially situated' (Harding, 1993: 54) and, as such, there can be no claim of objectivity or neutrality; or, as Haraway says, there is no 'god trick' (Haraway, 1988). This is clearly evidenced in the recording, reading and interpreting of documented knowledge claims about Black women. Furthermore, the function and production of oppressive, socially-situated knowledge claims work to undermine the position and legitimacy of Black feminist scholarship. What becomes apparent is that the practice of close reading as a method is both part of the problem that is being challenged and forms part of the political challenge that confronts oppressive readings of people. This chapter examines the inherent tension involved in the practice of re-reading Lorde and, in doing so, makes direct application of the inherent tensions involved in the activism of Black feminist theory.

'"Good" literary criticism, the only worthwhile kind, implies an act, a literary signature or counter-signature, an inventive experience of language, *in* language, an inscription of the act of reading in the field of the text that is read' (Derrida, 1992a: 52; emphasis in original). The act of re-reading Lorde is an inventive experience because each re-reading is different. No re-reading is the same and, as such, each re-reading is a new re-reading. The predicament is that of how to establish and communicate any sense of a comprehensible, coherent re-reading of Lorde when each re-reading destabilizes any notion of an 'established', and in doing so, contests any

notion of an 'established'. The predicament takes on a particular significance in relation to the activism of liberation theories and communication
of messages designed to create coalitions of resistance to oppression. In
other words, the questions become: how can the impossibility of a unified,
established communication work to form the possibility of a unified, established political resistance? How can the call to political, collective action
that is reiterated throughout Lorde's text be possible when reiteration
produces inevitable fissures? How can there be 'the transformation of
silence into language and action' (Lorde, 1977: 40) in the condition of the
impossibility of language? The gap between the iterated and the reiterated
in the term 're-reading', represented by the hyphen, is a preoccupation of
this book investigated through intertextual (re-)readings of Lorde.

In contesting any notion of an established, unified singularity, the space
and place between the iterated and the reiterated contest an established,
unified singularity of author intention. Derrida explains that:

> What holds for the receiver holds also, for the same reasons, for the
> sender or the producer. To write is to produce a mark that will consti-
> tute a sort of machine which is productive in turn, and which my future
> disappearance will not, in principle, hinder in its functioning, offering
> things and itself to be read and to be rewritten. When I say "my future
> disappearance" [*disparition*: also, demise, *trans.*], it is in order to
> render this proposition more immediately acceptable. I ought to be able
> to say my disappearance, pure and simple, my nonpresence in general,
> for instance the nonpresence of my intention of saying something
> meaningful [*mon vouloir-dire, mon intention-de-signification*], of my
> wish to communicate, from the emission or production of the mark.
> For a writing to be a writing it must continue to "act" and to be read-
> able even when what is called the author of the writing no longer
> answers for what he has written, for what he seems to have signed ...
> (Derrida, 1972: 8; parentheses and italics in original)

The dialectic here is that Lorde's 'nonpresence' to herself renders her
'mark' (written and verbal enunciations) and her intention in the 'mark'
impossible to ascertain, but, and here is the bone of contention, the act of
writing and (re-)reading relies on some kind of recognition of the 'mark'.
Derrida summarizes the dialectic as: 'What is re-markable about the mark
includes the margin within the mark. The line delineating the margin can
therefore never be determined rigorously, it is never pure and simple. The
mark is re-markable in that it "is" also its margin' (Derrida, 1977: 70).

The predicament of the margin, border and boundary is a recurrent theme
within critical psychology or, indeed, any liberatory theory. A critical

analysis of the aporia of margins provokes a critical re-working of the politics of being on the margins, marginalized and marginality. Furthermore, it provokes a re-thinking of the position, function and production of the idea of 'centre'. Parker takes up this issue in relation to critical psychology's critique of traditional psychology, and the ways in which knowledge is represented and positioned as inside or outside of the centre of this discipline are a feature of the relationship between knowledge and power:

> Here we encounter a question often asked of critical psychologists, and which deserves answer. How can this critical reflection be a contribution to knowledge? We must look again at our map, for this question reveals something about the map traditional psychologists use, and the ways in which they assume that they are at the centre. Psychologists imagine that they are starting their journeys from dry land, and they return to their institutions after exploring strange uncharted waters to make sense of what they have found. Traditional psychology likes to think that it is the one centre for theories of the mind. Debate about psychology outside traditional frameworks, or scepticism about any psychological framework would not, then, be seen as a contribution to knowledge. Critical psychologists disagree, on two counts. First of all there are always multiple centres for meaning if there are 'centres' at all, and it is always possible to take apart an intellectual system and trace its component parts to different ideological representations or to the interests of certain social groups. This is the case for all 'psychologies', even the ostensibly most radical, and every careful analysis adds to our critical psychological knowledge about the interrelationship between culture and theory, and the interrelationship between theory and practice.
>
> (Parker, 1999: 11–12)

Re-reading Lorde is both to occupy the margin and to make use of the margin so that the impossible, the unavailable and the fissures of re-reading Black feminist theoretical communications are the conditions of the activism of Black feminist theory. From this perspective, energy can be directed away from establishing a correct (re-)reading or fixing of the intention of political texts – a source of so many divisions, exclusions and replication of hierarchical positions that have haunted, and continue to haunt, political movements for social justice. Rather, energy should be re-directed towards the situation and experience of instability as a site of political subversion. Spivak explains that 'the absence of sender and receiver is the *positive* condition of possibility of "communication"' (Spivak, 1980: 80; emphasis in original), and therefore, effective resistance to oppression depends on effective communication.

Speaking out about the activism of Black feminist theory

Lorde had trouble speaking:

> Even one intelligible word was a very rare event for me. And although the doctors at the clinic had clipped the little membrane under my tongue so I was no longer tongue-tied, and had assured my mother that I was not retarded, she still had her terrors and her doubts. She was genuinely happy for any possible alternative to what she was afraid might be a dumb child.
>
> (Lorde, 1996: 14)

> My mother had a special and secret relationship with words, taken for granted as language because it was always there. I did not speak until I was four.
>
> (Lorde, 1996: 21)

> I was very inarticulate as a youngster. I couldn't speak. I didn't speak until I was five, in fact, not really, until I started reading and writing poetry. I used to speak in poetry. I would read poems, and I would memorize them. People would say, well what do you think, Audre. What happened to you yesterday? And I would recite a poem ...
>
> (Evans, 1979: 71)

These excerpts bring together a range of issues concerned with the act of speaking that are relevant to the act of declaring or speaking out about the activism of Black feminist theory. A close re-reading of Lorde's words here indicates: speech as a marker of what it is to be a legitimate, intelligent human being; speech as 'taken for granted' and 'always there' while holding the quality of the 'secret'; and the relationship between speech, writing, conventions of speech and the unconventional chaos of poetry. John Austin maintained that: 'Once we realize that what we have to study is *not* the sentence but the issuing of an utterance in a speech-situation, there can hardly be any longer a possibility of not seeing that stating is performing an act' (Austin, 1975: 139; emphasis in original). The act being performed is the creation of a social and psychic reality within a social context.

This framing draws on the theory of the speech act (Austin, 1975; Searle, 1969, 1975) developed by Judith Butler into the feminist theory of performativity. Butler explains that '[w]ithin speech act theory, a perfor-mative is that discursive practice that enacts or produces that which it names' (Butler, 1993a: 13). The implications of this for the 'excitable speech' (Butler, 1997b) of the activism of Black feminist theory include the following factors:

- the situation of Black women, in every sense of the word, is not a product of nature, but a product of discursive practice;
- discursive practices are unstable social, historical, cultural, economic and political artefacts (Burr, 1995: 3–5);
- performativity is not a one-off act, but works through repetitive re-inscriptions (Butler, 1999: xv);
- the contingent instability of the contextualized artefact, the production of communication and the inevitable space represented in the hyphen in the term 're-inscription' are opportunities for subversion;
- the opportunities in the space between each enactment of the declaration of the activism of Black feminist theory are a chance for the insurrection of the laws of discursive practice (especially when those practices subjugate Black women).

There is a need to re-work reductionist centre/margin perspectives. The 're-markable' (Derrida, 1977: 70) Lorde as the margin and the decentring of logos as utterance, text, author and declarer of Black feminist theory productively messes with neat centre/margin configurations of 'master territories' (Minh-ha, 1991). The relationship between speaking, knowledge and work is articulated by Ahmed in the following way: 'considering the epistemic dimensions of speaking will demonstrate the links between representation and broader relationships of production' (Ahmed, 2000: 61). Thus, 'who speaks?', 'who hears?' and 'who is knowing, here?' (Ahmed, 2000: 61) constitute questions that are fundamental to the production of, and productions within, any critical analysis of the psy-complex.

Audre Lorde: the aporia of positionality

In the following excerpts from *Zami* (1996), Lorde takes up the conundrum of location, space and margins as she tries to negotiate a subject position:

> I did not like the tail of the Y hanging down below the line in Audrey, and would always forget to put it on ... We were given special short wide notebooks to write in, with very widely spaced lines on yellow paper. They looked like my sister's music notebooks. We were also given thick black crayons to write with ... I knew quite well that crayons were not what you wrote with, and music books were definitely not what you wrote in. I raised my hand. When the teacher asked me what

I wanted, I asked for some regular paper to write on and a pencil. That was my undoing. "We don't have any pencils here," I was told.

(Lorde, 1996: 14–15)

I bent my head down close to the desk that smelled like old spittle and rubber erasers, and on that ridiculous yellow paper with those laughably wide spaces I printed my best AUDRE. I had never been too good at keeping between straight lines no matter what their width, so it slanted down across the page something like this:

A
  U
    D
      R
        E

The notebooks were short and there was no more room for anything else on that page. So I turned the page and went over, and wrote again, earnestly and laboriously, biting my lip,

L
  O
    R
      D
        E ...

(Lorde, 1996: 15)

These excerpts show that from as early as the age of four years old, Lorde was engaged in:

The question as to when one should "mark" oneself (in terms of ethnicity, age, class, gender, or sexuality for example) and when one should adamantly refuse such markings ... For answers to this query remain bound to the specific location, context, circumstance, and history of the subject at a given moment. Here, positionings are radically transitional and mobile.

(Minh-ha, 2011: 51; parentheses in original)

This book traces the ways in which Lorde takes up Minh-ha's question of when to 'mark' oneself and when to 'refuse such markings'. The point is that this question is fundamental to any political resistance to oppressive social constructions.

Although positionings are mobile, mobility does not provide an escape or relief from the aporia of positionality. Lorde's position of being outside the lines of demarcation on the 'very widely spaced lines on yellow paper' (Lorde, 1996: 14) remains a position in itself, and that position is defined in relation to, and constituted by, the specific location, context and circumstance of 'that ridiculous yellow paper with those laughably wide spaces' (Lorde, 1996: 15) and the 'thick black crayons to write with' (Lorde, 1996: 14). Thus, a critical analysis of the claims of position, movement and undoing of position in the metanarrative of all political movements for social justice is vital.

Implicated

Daniela Caselli dismantles the inevitable tension in the following way:

> The metanarrative assertion, however, also presents itself as an authoritative claim, as if it could escape the very game of which it is part and could guarantee the reality or unreality of what is written. Although there is no ground to decide what is artificial, since the claim belongs to the same fictional world that it denounces, the rhetoric creates the illusion that, by judging what the narrator has just said, it stands on a higher ground. The metanarrative statement occupies an ambiguous position, as it is implicated in the narrative it criticises and it also stands above it in order to judge it.
>
> (Caselli, 2005: 105)

In other words, regardless of both the methodology we use and the political positions we adopt, it is an inescapable fact that we are all always implicated. We are implicated because it is impossible to stand outside of discourse. In the task of 'judging', and in the questioning of 'artificial' fictions of the madness and misery of Black women, the question becomes: how can the metanarrative of critical psychology, the activism of Black feminist theory or, indeed, any theory of liberation present authoritative claims (and they need to be authoritative in the face of women's denied authority, and in particular, in the face of a racist, homophobic patriarchy that denies the authority of Black women) while being part of the 'game'? This is the predicament of positionality: all positions are mutually contingent and constitutive, and as such, all positions are implicated.

In terms of race, the question for critical race theory, Black feminist theory, post-colonial theory and for Lorde is: 'how can the black subject posit a full and sufficient self in a language in which blackness is a sign of absence?' (Gates, 1986: 218). Gates' query is particularly relevant for two reasons: first, because it can be applied both to race and gender, and the application takes on increased significance in terms of the intersectionality of race, gender and other categories of identity that are constituted as a sign of absence; and second, because the problem he articulates establishes that the notion of 'absence' in itself does not provide an escape from the aporia of positionality. Thus, Gates enables a more nuanced understanding of the aporia of positionality, whereby neither mobility nor absence provides an escape.

More specifically, the question is: how does Lorde or, indeed, any political praxis grapple with this ambiguous, implicated position? Indeed, the production of any praxis of emancipation is the question of, and a questioning of, positions. In this context, it is a question of how I position Lorde and am (re-)positioned by Lorde. Here, I am beginning to understand something of what Spivak wrote in the first paragraph of 'Can the Subaltern Speak?': 'although I will attempt to foreground the precariousness of my position throughout, I know such gestures can never suffice' (Spivak, 1988: 271).

Black feminist methodology

This book is a gesture of working with Lorde, and it is a gesture of putting Lorde to work. Drawing on scholarship including, for example, post-colonial, literary, Black feminist and deconstructionist theory, this multi-disciplinary, pedagogical intervention juxtaposes a range of standpoints and theoretical approaches. In terms of methodology, this is an intersection of 'interlocking and mutually reinforcing' (Nash, 2008: 3), constitutive approaches. The objective is to provide a new critical, close re-reading of Lorde produced out of her 'specific location, context, circumstance, and history' (Minh-ha, 2011: 51). The methodology juxtaposes those given moments of production with the given moments of current feminist debates. An objective of this methodology is to transgress boundaries across a temporal and spatial spectrum. Furthermore, 'the specific location, context, circumstance, and history of the subject at a given moment' (Minh-ha, 2011: 51) apply both to author and reader to produce particular and shifting re-readings at any given time, space and place. Lorde performs what Minh-ha (2011) calls 'the boundary event' and, in doing so, Lorde enables us to think about, and to narrate, the happenings of the boundary.

This book adopts the concept of 'the boundary event' as a methodology and, in doing so, it performs a theoretical 'boundary event'. It is an example of content and method intersecting. It will become evident that the subject under analysis, and the method to investigate the subject under analysis, are mutually constitutive. Indeed, I would argue that the intersection of method, analysis and content is a consistent structure that constitutes all scholarship, research and practice. Because 'the space and place we inhabit produce us' (Probyn, 2003: 294), space and place produce methodology.

For example, the space and place of aporia, the dialectic, intersectionality and the matrix of domination simultaneously constitute the subject under analysis, and the methodology for analysis.

In relation to the activism of Black feminist theory, it is no coincidence that this method is as an organic process, given that:

> Black feminist politics by its very nature exists right at the intersection of several issues that are located in Black women's experiences. And since experience is also ideologically produced, and Black women's experience is what Black women's writing purports to express, we are also simultaneously examining ideological, discursive positions of some Black women who are writers.

> (Boyce Davies, 1994: 30)

The methodology arising from the experience of engaging with the activism of Black feminist theory is contingent upon, and constituted by, a number of intersecting factors that include:

1   The fact that 'Black feminist criticisms, then, perhaps more than many of the other feminisms, can be a praxis where the theoretical positions and the criticism interact with the lived experience' (Boyce Davies, 1994: 55). It is the interaction of theory with lived experience that creates the methodology of Black feminist criticism. More specifically, a core aspect of the project of this book is to expose, re-claim and assert the theoretical position of Lorde's work – a task that includes the dialectic of examining the suppression of that position, while contesting that suppression. Collins explains that:

> This dialectic of oppression and activism, the tension between the suppression of African-American women's ideas and our intellectual activism in the face of that suppression, constitutes the politics of U.S. Black feminist thought. More important, understanding this dialectical relationship is critical in assessing how U.S. Black feminist thought – its core themes, epistemological significance, and connections to domestic and transnational Black feminist practice – is fundamentally embedded in a political context that has challenged its very right to exist.

> (Collins, 2000: 3–4)

2   Barbara Christian states: 'I think we need to read the works of our writers in our various ways and remain open to the intricacies of the intersection of language, class, race, and gender in the literature' (Christian, 1987: 13). For me, being 'open to the intricacies of the intersection' is a

methodology and produces a methodology. Lorde identifies being 'open' as a use of the erotic, 'whether it is dancing, building a bookcase, writing a poem, examining an idea' (Lorde, 1978: 56–7). In being 'open' to examining the ideas of Black feminist literature, I realize, and '[i]t feels right to me' (Lorde, 1978: 56), that Lorde's Black feminist 'uses of the erotic' are a methodology. It is a methodology that stands in defiance of scientific, empirical research methods. In other words: 'Beyond the superficial, the considered phrase, "It feels right to me," acknowledges the strength of the erotic into a true knowledge, for what that means is the first and most powerful guiding light toward any understanding' (Lorde, 1978: 56). In contrast to Western measures of validity and reliability, the activism of Black feminist methodology is an erotic process of feeling. Thus, 'the suppression of Black women's intellectual traditions has made this process of feeling one's way an unavoidable epistemological stance for Black women intellectuals' (Collins, 2000: 19). I propose that consideration of, 'It feels right to me', provides a methodology for negotiating 'a channel between the "high theoretical" and the "suspicious of all theories"' (Boyce Davies, 1994: 43). The method of opening the 'high theoretical' to the intricacies and suppression of Black women's experience, work and voice keeps suspicion alive, while not allowing suspicion to destroy that which is useful theoretically.

3   The methodology is contingent upon, and constituted through, the grassroots feminist work that is central to my living: for example, working in Manchester, Oxford and Trafford Rape Crisis centres, engagement with asylum-seekers and refugee women, and numerous community-based education projects. Lorde's own involvement in grassroots feminist activism included the creation of 'Sisters in Support of Sisters in South Africa' (SISA) (Kraft, 1986: 152) under apartheid, and the founding of the 'Kitchen Table Press' with Barbara Smith in the late 1980s (Cavin, 1983: 106). The dialogical relationship between experience, practice and scholarship produces the methodology of the activism of Black feminist theory, where the *how to do*, and the *doing*, of the project intersect. Boyce Davies makes the point that:

> Scholarship and theoretical writing by Black women, because they exist in an academic context, have become distant and removed from the day-to-day lives of most people. But it is not only the fact of the critic distantly removed from the people which is the issue, but the ways in which Black women as writers, academics, teachers, who live lives of multiple oppression, still end up paradoxically unintelligible to those who are unschooled in critical discourses and also to those who are.
>
> (Boyce Davies, 1994: 36)

Throughout this book, I make a concerted effort to transfer the text of Black feminist critical theory from the page to the day-to-day struggles of Black feminist activism. I agree with Boyce Davies that 'Black feminist critics have to make a concerted effort ... to do community work whenever/wherever possible' (Boyce Davies, 1994: 36). For example, in Chapter 3, Lorde's statement that 'Black feminism is not white feminism in blackface' (Lorde, 1979b: 60) is used to examine the necessity of Black-women-only reflective spaces and specific Black-women-only service provision. In Chapter 4, 'The Aporetics of Intersectionality' form a basis to analyse the emotional impact of 'integrat[ing] all the parts of who I am' (Lorde, 1980a: 120). Examination of the 'psychological toll' (The Combahee River Collective, 1977: 266) of embodied intersectionality is applied to the struggles encountered in collective-working and the experience of engaging with Black feminist texts.

Politics of pronouns: the matter of who is speaking

The matter of who is speaking, and the predicaments of availability and unavailability of the author within any text (including case notes, records, diagnostic manuals of classification, biographies, testimonies, speeches and political essays), are prime examples of the relevance and application of critical literary theories of deconstruction to applied practices. This disrupts the idea that methods belong to particular disciplines and professions that serve to re-inscribe regulatory borders that inhibit critical analysis.

'In fact, however, all discourses endowed with the author function do possess this plurality of self' (Foucault, 1969: 112). This plurality arises because the pronoun 'I' of the author 'refers to an individual without an equivalent who, in a determined place and time, completed a certain task' (Foucault, 1969: 112). In other words, Lorde, as author, was never available either to us or to herself. This is not just because she is physically dead; equivalence is disrupted because '[t]he knowing self is partial in all its guises, never finished, whole' (Haraway, 1988: 288). In turn, the intentions of Lorde, as author, are never available even when the author 'speaks to tell the work's meaning, the obstacles encountered, the results obtained, and the remaining problems' (Foucault, 1969: 112). The implications of this are far reaching in that it makes questionable any claim of knowing another; for example, it destabilizes the legitimacy of patient case notes as a basis of knowing.

Furthermore, the self/selves of a pronoun, whether in the form of author or reader, is/are always 'situated in the field of already existing or yet-to-appear' (Foucault, 1969: 112). This is demonstrated in the methodology and content of 'my' text, where the construction of 'my' is through a re-reading, application and citation of multiple authors 'without an equivalent who, in a determined place and time, completed a certain task' (Foucault, 1969: 112). In other words, as the author of the text of this book, I am as unavailable (to myself and to you as the reader) as the authors within the text of the book. This dynamic takes on particular significance when the 'without an equivalent' is manufactured into a totalizing equivalent, as is the case with texts written by or about Black women. Foucault's point is that the 'determined place and time' function to produce the situation of 'without an equivalent'. In short, the time and place of writing five minutes ago are no longer available and, thus, the author of five minutes ago is also no longer available (Benveniste, 1961). However, in the case of texts written by or about Black women, the opposite occurs: the notion of a 'determined place and time' is used to fix and solidify the subject and content of the writing, resulting in essentialist configurations of authenticity and homogeneity.

Close re-reading of the use of pronouns in texts written by or about Black women indicates the ways in which semantics operate as instruments of connection and disconnection. Lorde's writing shifts constantly back and forth from the first to the third person, including frequent use of collective pronouns. These shifting positions are performative of her claims about difference, subjectivity and identity. The fluctuations between different pronouns create a polyrhythmic effect that enables different signifiers of identity and subjectivity to be played around with. Lorde grew up within a household of 'that Grenadian poly-language' (Lorde, 1996: 7), where '[t]he sensual content of life was masked and cryptic, but attended in well-coded phrases' (Lorde, 1996: 22). For example:

> We were never dressed too lightly, but rather "in next kin to nothing." *Neck skin to nothing?* Impassable and impossible distances were measured by the distance "from Hog to Kick 'em Jenny." *Hog? Kick 'em Jenny?* … A mild reprimand was accompanied not by a slap on the behind, but a "smack on the backass," or on the "bamsy." You sat on your "bam-bam," but anything between your hipbones and upper thighs was consigned to the "lower-region."
>
> (Lorde, 1996: 21; emphasis in original)

Here, Lorde locates the 'well-coded' (Lorde, 1996: 22) within the poly-rhythms of polyvocality and poly-language. It could be argued that Lorde exposes the politics of signifying practices, and the relationship between location and speech – whether that is the location of the private domestic sphere, the location of being Black and/or the location of the 'other tongues' (Boyce Davies, 1994: 153). The relation between location and speech can be seen in the use of pronouns. Alistair Pennycook explains that pronouns 'are in fact very complex and political words, always raising difficult issues of who is being represented. There is, therefore, never an unproblematic "we" or "you" or "they" or "I" or "he/she"' (Pennycook, 1994: 173). These difficult issues become more pronounced when it is a Black woman who is being represented. Using the pronoun 'we', June Jordan succinctly states that '[t]he problem is that we are saying *language*, but really dealing with power' (Jordan, 1972: 35; emphasis in original). The conscious political use of pronouns within Black feminism functions to disrupt racist, homophobic, patriarchal positionings. For example, Collins explains:

> ... I argue that Black women intellectuals best contribute to a Black women's group standpoint by using their experiences as situated knowers. To adhere to this epistemological tenet required that, when appropriate, I reject the pronouns "they" and "their" when describing U.S. Black women and our ideas and replace these terms with the terms "we," "us," and "our." Using the distancing terms "they" and "their" when describing my own group and our experiences might enhance both my credentials as a scholar and the credibility of my arguments in some academic settings. But by taking this epistemological stance that reflects my disciplinary training as a sociologist, I invoke standards of certifying truth about which I remain ambivalent.
>
> (Collins, 2000: 19)

Historical amnesia

The activism of Black feminist theory tracks and resists the 'historical amnesia that keeps us working to invent the wheel every time we have to go to the store for bread' (Lorde, 1980a: 117). In 'A Burst of Light' (1988), Lorde provides a personal and poignant reflection that brings in an added, tangential dimension to the waste of 'working to invent the wheel' (Lorde, 1980a: 117). In 'A Burst of Light', Lorde reflects on the loss and isolation that not knowing about the 'wheel' gives rise to:

> I often think of Angelina Weld Grimké dying alone in an apartment in New York City in 1958 while I was a young Black Lesbian struggling in isolation at Hunter College, and I think of what it could have meant in terms of sisterhood and survival for each one of us to have known of the other's existence: for me to have had her words and her wisdom, and for her to have known I needed them!
>
> (Lorde, 1988: 288)

The point I need to emphasize is that the text of this book is a deliberate and purposeful intervention to confront the 'neither accidental nor benign'

(Collins, 2000: 3) 'historical amnesia' of Lorde's work that is representative of the travesty of suppressing the scholarship of Black feminism. It is a work of re-membering.

I want to highlight three mutually contingent points in relation to 'historical amnesia' that recur in different guises. I introduce the first point with a piece written by June Jordan (1982). Jordan describes an encounter that took place during a Black Sisters Speak-Out, where:

> ... one of the women announced that we should realize our debt to the great Black women who have preceded us in history. "We are here," she said, "because of the struggle of women like," and here her sentence broke down. She tried again. "We have come this far because of all the Black women who fought for us like, like ... " and, here, only one name came to her mouth: "Sojourner Truth!" she exclaimed, clearly relieved to think of it, but also embarrassed because she couldn't keep going. "And," she tried to continue, nevertheless, "the other Black women like ... " but here somebody in the audience spoke to her rescue, by calling aloud the name Harriet Tubman. At this point I interrupted to observe that now we had *two* names for *482* years of our Afro-American history. "What about Mary McLeod Bethune?" somebody else ventured at last. "That's three!" I remarked, in the manner of a referee: "Do we have a fourth?" There was a silence. Thoroughly embarrassed, the first woman looked at me and said, "Listen. I could come up with a whole list of Black women if my life depended on it." "Well," I had to tell her, "It does."
>
> (Jordan, 1982: 133; ellipses and emphasis in original)

The first point is that resisting 'historical amnesia' goes beyond 'the waste of an amnesia that robs us of lessons of the past' (Lorde, 1982: 139), and it goes beyond 'having to repeat and relearn the same old lessons over and over' (Lorde, 1980a: 117). My first point is that resisting 'historical amnesia' is vital because our life depends upon it and, as such, it opens up a range of issues about the place and production of the subject and subjectivity. 'Historical amnesia' stands in direct relation to the position of Black women and what Black women produce in society. It is an issue about recognition (or not) of the existence (or not) of Black women, their experiences and what they produce.

Thus, it is possible to re-read 'historical amnesia' as a manifestation of the 'false and treacherous connections' (Lorde, 1980a: 115) that Lorde refers to because 'we have no patterns for relating across our human differences as equals' (Lorde, 1980a: 115), which leads 'many Black women into testifying against themselves' (Lorde, 1980a: 121). This is articulated by Jordan:

> From looking around the room I knew there were Black women right there who face critical exposure to bodily assault, alcoholic mothers, and racist insults and graffiti in the dorms. I knew that the academic curriculum omitted the truth of their difficult lives. I knew that they certainly would not be found welcome in the marketplace after they got their degrees. But the insistent concern was more intimate and more pitiful and more desperate than any of those threatening conditions might suggest. The abject plea of those Black women students was ruthlessly minimal: "If you see me, you could say, '*Hi*.'" Let me know that you see me; let me know I exist. Never mind a conversation between us, but, please, if you see me, you could say "*Hi*."
>
> (Jordan, 1982: 133–4; emphasis in original)

The second point is articulated by Brah and Phoenix, who explain that:

> By revisiting these historical developments, we do not wish to suggest that the past unproblematically provides an answer to the present. On the contrary, we would wish to learn from and build upon these insights through critique so that they can shed new light on current predicaments.
>
> (Brah & Phoenix, 2004: 75)

Indeed, it is precisely due to the fact that re-visiting Lorde does not unproblematically provide answers to current predicaments that makes her a sharp critical lens of analysis for the present. In other words, it is the encounter with unresolved tensions that yields the most fruitful opportunities for productive thinking.

The third point is the need to track and resist the urge to 'romanticize our past in order to be aware of how it seeds our present' (Lorde, 1982: 139) – an urge that is particularly seductive in relation to the iconic figures.

Suspicion of Lorde, the icon

The significance of this point is that 'an iconicity that is altogether too good to be true' (Suleri, 1992: 250) blurs critical analysis, not least because it freezes the subject. In other words, in relation to Lorde, for example, the effect of 'Audre-ism' (Joseph, 2009: 249) and elevation to the status of 'Shero' (J.B. Cole, 2009: 231) could work to foreclose the audacity of any questioning, dissatisfaction, disappointment or disagreement with 'the most revered, powerful, and influential African American feminist writer/activist of the twentieth century' (Guy-Sheftall, 2009: 253). Suleri warns that:

> ... the embarrassed privilege granted to racially encoded feminism does indeed suggest a rectitude that could be its own theoretical undoing. The concept of the postcolonial itself is too frequently robbed of historical specificity in order to function as a preapproved allegory for any mode of discursive contestation. The coupling of *postcolonial* with *woman*, however, almost inevitably leads to the simplicities that underlie unthinking celebrations of oppression, elevating the racially female voice into a metaphor for "the good." Such metaphoricity cannot exactly be called essentialist, but it certainly functions as an impediment to a reading that attempts to look beyond obvious questions of good and evil.
>
> (Suleri, 1992: 250; emphasis in original)

We would do well to heed Suleri's warning in the current attention towards Lorde, who now seems to be in vogue. For example, 2004 saw the publication of De Veaux's acclaimed biography of Lorde and *Conversations with Audre Lorde*, edited by Wylie Hall. In 2005, the University of Louisville used a donation of one million dollars to create the 'Audre Lorde Chair in Race, Class, Gender, and Sexuality' that was filled in 2007 (Guy-Sheftall, 2009: 259). In 2009, the Spellman Archives, featuring Lorde's papers, was opened to the public and *I Am Your Sister: Collected and Unpublished Writings of Audre Lorde* (Byrd *et al.*, 2009) was published. 2012 saw the release of the multi award-winning film, *Audre Lorde – The Berlin Years 1984 to 1992*, that has travelled across the USA and Europe. In addition, the number of conference symposiums, keynotes, blogs[1] and references to the influence of Lorde are evidence of current interest in her work: for example, in the work of Ahmed (2009, 2010, 2012) and her trendsetting phrase, 'feminist killjoys'.

Although this turn to Lorde is gratifying, I hold Suleri's position of suspicion, articulated vividly by duCille's use of Moraga's metaphor of a bridge:

> Both black women writers and the black feminist critics who have brought them from the depths of obscurity into the ranks of the academy have been such bridges. The trouble is that, as Moraga points out, bridges get walked on over and over and over again. This sense of being a bridge – of being walked on and passed over, of being used up and burnt out, of having to "publish while perishing", as some have described their situations – seems to be a part of the human condition of many black women scholars.
>
> (duCille, 1994: 254)

It would seem that the more Black feminist scholarship is welcomed into the fold of academia, the more vigilant Black feminists need to be about the function, dangers and consequences of this welcome. We have nothing to be grateful for.

'Historical amnesia' functions in two mutually constitutive directions in terms of what is remembered and what is forgotten. The point is that both what is remembered and what is forgotten pose a threat to the existence of Black women, and to what Black women produce, not least because what is remembered and what is forgotten have the potential to undermine the resources that Black women have access to in relation to the development and survival of a sense of sisterhood. The punch line is, as Jordan (1982), Lorde (1980a, 1988) and Suleri (1992) make clear, that this is performed both in and through Black women themselves, 'coated in myths, stereo-types, and expectations from the outside, definitions not our own' (Lorde, 1983a: 170), so that Black women become the mechanism for what is both remembered and forgotten in the service of a racist, homophobic patriarchy.

Black feminist theory: the function of absence and presence

The idea of 'breaking bread' (hooks & West, 1991) with contemporary issues is a method of demonstrating the relevance and translation of Lorde as a theoretical lens to critically analyse the production of Black women, and what Black women produce. The paradox is that the scholarship that follows Lorde enables an enhanced, nuanced, detailed re-reading, but also begs the question of 'epistemic violence' (Spivak, 1988: 280), appropriation and fore-closure of her work in particular, and Black feminist scholarship in general. Hence, what is 'post' about post-colonialism and post-modernism? (Ata Aidoo, 1991: 152). Boyce Davies explains that in the 'post', 'we are auto-matically interpellated in ideologies of posting or postponing' (Boyce Davies, 1994: 83). Rather than asking what is 'post', Mukherjee (1990) re-frames the question to ask, '*Whose Post-Colonialism and Whose Postmodernism?*' The question moves the debate on from the intersecting issues of the production and position of Black feminist theory to an inquiry about:

- the suppression of Black feminist theory as a manoeuvre of coloniza-tion, where acts of appropriation are fundamental to maintaining racist, homophobic, patriarchal supremacy;
- the ways in which the suppression of Black feminist theory is disa-vowed and, just as importantly, the function of that disavowal in rela-tion to the ambivalence present in all manoeuvres of appropriation.

The tracking of the manoeuvres of appropriation is tricky because it involves much more than a tracking of the binary of inclusion/exclusion. In other words, tracking where, when and why the work of Lorde in particular, and the work of Black feminist theory in general, is included and excluded in contemporary scholarship, reading lists and citations could produce quantitative data of strategic use, but it misses something. First, the function of the absence and presence is missed; actually, to be more specific, the production of the binary, and what the binary functions to produce, is at risk of being occluded by the fixation on the binary. For example, it could evade an analysis of 'the rules of recognition' (Bhabha, 1994: 110) that determine the basis of inclusion and exclusion of Black feminist theory within contemporary scholarship. Secondly, the binary of absence/presence misses the event of the space in between. The point is that missing the in-between space renders that space unacknowledged, so that the happenings in the event of the boundary are foreclosed.

The same points could be applied to the absence/presence of Black women's services that I have been engaged with in Rape Crisis centres. The analysis can be broadened out to any specific service provision for Black, Asian and Minoritized Ethnic peoples located within a general service or, indeed, located within a racist, homophobic patriarchy. For example, interrogation about both the number of calls taken on a Black women's helpline, and the ratio of Black women within an organization – as well as tracking the number of times a Black woman's (as service-user and service-provider) voice is present or absent, recognized, unrecognized or misrecognized, acknowledged or unacknowledged – could produce quantitative data of strategic use, but it misses something. What it misses is an inquiry into what a Black women's service functions to contain within an organization. It misses an inquiry into what is happening in the in-between space of the binary of absence/presence. It misses an inquiry into what the fixation on the binary functions to produce and what produces the fixation in the first place. Starting and ending with the binary of absence/presence is a disavowal of the anxiety of existing with the construction of the 'other'.

Hybridity

I find Bhabha's (1994) idea of hybridity a particularly useful analytic lens to think about the production and function of the position of Lorde's work specifically, and the activism of Black feminist theory in general:

> If the effect of colonial power is seen to be the *production* of hybridiza-
> tion rather than the noisy command of colonialist authority or the silent

repression of native traditions, then an important change of perspective occurs. The ambivalence at the source of traditional discourses on authority enables a form of subversion, founded on undecidability that turns the discursive conditions of dominance into the grounds of intervention. It is traditional academic wisdom that the presence of authority is properly established through the non-exercise of private judgement and the exclusion of reasons in conflict with the authoritative reason. The recognition of authority, however, requires a validation of its source that must be immediately, even intuitively, apparent – "You have that in your countenance which I would fain call master" – and held in common (rules of recognition). What is left unacknowledged is the paradox of such a demand for proof and the resulting ambivalence for positions of authority.

(Bhabha, 1994: 112; emphasis and parentheses in original)

Collins' (2000: 15) analysis of the *not silenced*, but *not too noisy* positioning of Sojourner Truth's contribution to Black feminist critical theory provides a good example of how this tactic of 'hybridization' works. Although Sojourner Truth's (1851) speech, 'Ain't I a Woman?', has not been silenced, as evidenced by frequent citations of her question in texts, conference speeches and political activism, neither has it been accredited with the 'noisy command' of her intellectual prowess, as evidenced by the complexity of the philosophical, theoretical and linguistic movements within the speech.

From a political perspective that sees Lorde's work and Black feminist discourse in the obscuring shadow of hybridization, it is possible to see Foucault's power/knowledge relation at work. 'Hybridization' would be a procedure by which 'the production of discourse is at once controlled, selected, organised and redistributed' (Foucault, 1981: 52). This 'important change of perspective' that Bhabha (1994: 112) refers to is taken up within this book as a method of close re-reading to track the implicated grounds of hybridity that Lorde and Black feminism stand on. This perspective takes seriously Mbembe's caution that:

... domination is a regime that involves not just control but conviviality, even connivance – as shown by the constant compromises, the small tokens of fealty ... individuals are constantly being trapped in a net of rituals that reaffirm tyranny, and in that these rituals, however minor, are intimate in nature.

(Mbembe, 2001: 66)

Bhabha (1994), Mbembe (2001) and Caselli (2005) bring a number of inter-connecting problematics to the table that are pivotal to this book:

- To what extent, how and why should Lorde be regarded 'critically as a problem, not a solution, as a sign to be interrogated, a locus of contra-dictions' (Carby, 1987: 15)?
- What strategies do Lorde and Black feminists use to grapple with the aporia of positionality?
- How do Lorde and Black feminists seek out possibilities for subversive manoeuvres in the in-between space of hybridity, as exemplified by Anzaldúa's (2007) redefining of the hybrid position in *Borderlands/La Frontera: The New Mestiza*?

Borderlands of the dialectic

Deconstructionist and post-colonial approaches reflected in Bhabha's expli-cation of 'hybridization' locate the space and possibility for subversion within the 'undecidability that turns the discursive conditions of dominance into the grounds of intervention' (Bhabha, 1994: 112). Speaking in relation to Lorde and the activism of Black feminist theory, I would contend that an aspect of the 'undecidability' is to be simultaneously implicated and subversive.

The borderlands of dialectic movement between the implicated and the subversive are difficult to occupy for a number of reasons: first, picking up on the metaphor of movement, occupation of the tension between the impli-cated and the subversive invokes a kind of motion sickness; second, occu-pation of movement between these tensions that constitute the dialectic entails giving up learnt strategies for coping with the symptoms of the motion sickness. It entails not resorting to resolving the movement within the dialectic. For example, staying within the dialectic means not resorting to learnt patterns for relating across difference (Lorde, 1980a: 115). The dialectic is neither complicity, inversion nor replication, nor is it a split position of an either/or. So, the dialectic is inherently a place of loss – loss of resolution, loss of stability, loss of security, loss of the decided and loss of the prior. However, this configuration is a trick because the notion of loss implies that resolution, stability, security, decidability and the prior existed to be lost.

The borderlands of the dialectic make me think of the name 'Rape Crisis' in a new light. The name is rooted historically and politically within the women's liberation movement (Brownmiller, 1993, 1999), and as such, remains the name, even though both a frequent reaction to, and the impact of, its enunciation are extremely uncomfortable. The word 'crisis' invokes the idea of something immediate, traumatic and overwhelming, and most people's association with the words 'rape crisis' is that of the crisis of a rape that has just happened. However, survivors who use Rape Crisis services speak about the emotional impact of rape as having no time-frame. In other words, the trauma of rape destabilizes time so that terms such as 'recent' and 'historic' rape have no bearing on women's lived experience (Garland, 1998; Herman, 1997). So, what is the crisis? The crisis is that which is found in the following borderlands: between silence and speaking out; between the contrasting constructions of 'victim' and 'survivor'; and between the patriarchal, reiterative, constitutive tools of abuse of power and those of feminist consciousness-raising. The crisis is the productive site of borderlands for feminist de-constituting and re-constituting of thinking and interventions about sexual violence.

Black feminist author function

This book is a literary textual analysis of the work of Lorde. The task of under-taking a literary textual analysis of the work of Lorde, and the methodology available within literary criticism to undertake this task, presents a set of tensions. These tensions potentially undermine the legitimacy of the very task this book sets out to perform.

Two key objectives support the theoretical scaffolding of this book: first, it seeks to perform an intervention in its own right of explicating the work of Lorde (1934–92), located by some as part of second-wave feminism; second, it seeks to assert Lorde's authorial legitimacy to intervene in current third-wave feminist, post-modernist and post-colonial preoccupations about difference.

However, theories of literary criticism found in current third-wave femi-nist, post-modernist and post-colonial thinking potentially disrupt the basis of the interventions of this book, so that they are actually undone. Barthes (1967, 1971) and Foucault (1969), for example, present a set of complex problematics where the function, position and existence of the author trouble the function, position and existence of the subject and subjectivity. Burke articulates the complexity in the following way:

> If knowledge itself, or what we take to be knowledge, is entirely intra-discursive, and if, as it is claimed, the subject has no an*chora*ge within discourse, then man as the subject of knowledge is thoroughly displaced and dislodged. Cognition and consciousness arise as intralin-guistic effects or metaphors, by-products, as it were, of a linguistic order that has evolved …
>
> (Burke, 2008: 14; emphasis in original)

These tensions are bound fast with the aporia of positionality and take on particular significance in conjunction with the political imperatives of Black feminist scholarship. The particular significance that I am alluding to is taken up by Boyce Davies' question: 'But how does this all shift once Black women are introduced into the discussion? I believe that questions of Black female subjectivity bring a more complex and heightened awareness to all theoretics' (Boyce Davies, 1994: 29).

Once Black feminist authorship and literature are introduced into the discussion, it provokes the following questions: how does Black feminist scholarship anchor a position whilst, simultaneously, being unanchored? How does Black feminist scholarship establish legitimacy and authority in the face of 'the death of the author' (Barthes, 1967)? How does Black feminism contend with the absence of author, when a key objective of Black feminism is to contest the absence of Black feminist authors and texts? How can 'the death of the author' and the corresponding death of the subject sit with Jordan's (1982: 133) conviction that our lives depend on naming, remembering, recognizing and acknowledging the lives, activism and theory of Black feminists?

Lorde is concerned with the absence of the Black female subject and Black feminist productions (including scholarship), and I am concerned with how Lorde takes up these absences. Let me be clear that I do not take *absence* to mean *not present*. This point is taken up by Lorde (1979c) in 'An Open Letter to Mary Daly' in response to Daly's (1978) book, *Gyn/ Ecology*,[2] where Lorde posits the presence of the Black female subject and her work as constituting an absence:

> So the question arises in my mind, Mary, do you ever really read the work of Black women? Did you ever read my words, or did you merely finger through them for quotations which you thought might valuably support an already conceived idea concerning some old and distorted connection between us?
>
> (Lorde, 1979c: 68)

The principles that Lorde articulates here, when read through Foucault's (1969) 'What Is an Author?', prompt a more nuanced set of questions than I have just asked. Foucault explains that:

> Doing so means overturning the traditional problem, no longer raising the questions: How can a free subject penetrate the substance of things and give it meaning? How can it activate the rules of a language from within and thus give rise to the designs which are properly its own? Instead, these questions will be raised: How, under what conditions,

and in what forms can something like a subject appear in the order of discourse? What place can it occupy in each type of discourse, what functions can it assume, and by obeying what rules? In short, it is a matter of depriving the subject (or its substitute) of its role as originator, and of analyzing the subject as a variable and complex function of discourse.

(Foucault, 1969: 118)

Re-reading Lorde through the microscope of post-modernist literary criticism orientates the analysis through a set of interconnected themes that includes the conditions of representation of subjectivity, refracted through the prism of semiotics and intertextuality. The themes of intention, name and technologies of the self are an aspect of the production of 'the ideological figure by which one marks the manner in which we fear the proliferation of meaning' (Foucault, 1969: 119).

Question of the name

Although she was given the name 'Audrey Geraldine Lorde' by her parents, Lorde is not known by this name. Actually, no one can be known by their name, and this point is the basis for deconstructionist theories of the function of the name that are taken up within this book. Furthermore, this theoretical approach, when applied to the 'not knowing' of Black feminist scholarship and the treatment of the names of Black women writers, 'points to this "figure" that, at least in appearance, is outside it and antecedes it' (Foucault, 1969: 101). The 'name' becomes a methodology for understanding the historical and political outsider, and the 'excess' position of Black feminists and Black feminist theory. 'Black feminism is not white feminism in blackface' (Lorde, 1979b: 60) because it is outside of, and precedes, the name, the configuration of the name and the position of the name.

In particular, deconstructionist theories of the name enable close re-readings of the many names of Lorde. The list of names that Lorde uses include: Zami, Rey Domini (*Audre Lorde* in Latin) (Rich, 1979: 50) and 'Gambda Adisa, meaning Warrior: She Who Makes Her Meaning Known' (Reuman, 1997). In addition, certain titles or phrases, such as 'the sister outsider' (Byrd, 2009: 5) and 'Warrior Poet' (De Veaux, 2004), have become synonymous with the name, work and identity of Lorde. However, any equation of the bearer and the name of the bearer is problematic. Derrida proposes that:

> ... you will never be your name, you never have been, even when, and especially when you have answered to it. The name is made to do without the life of the bearer, and is therefore always the name of someone dead.
>
> (Derrida, 1987: 39)

The point Derrida is making here is that all names are outside of, and precede, the person/subject/object because any name refers and defers to an infinite web of historical, social and cultural contexts and concepts. A name carries death in the sense that any attempt to fix any name to any stable entity is impossible. Thus, a name signifies the demise of decidability, with all of the implications of mourning associated with bereavement. Any attempt to equate Lorde with 'the sister outsider' and 'Warrior Poet', *les amies* and African mythic Fon figures (such as Afrekete and MawuLisa) is 'always already' (Althusser, 1971) dead and lost.

At the age of four, Lorde 'did not like the tail of the Y hanging down below the line in Audrey, and would always forget to put it on' (Lorde, 1996: 14). Lorde explains that she 'used to love the evenness of AUDRELORDE' (Lorde, 1996: 14). Here, a close re-reading could interpret Lorde's description as invoking the spatial and temporal 'outside' and 'precedes' quality of a name that Derrida translates as the distinction between the name and the bearer of the name. A close re-reading could understand Lorde as invoking the 'drama of naming' (Derrida, 1992a: 187), where the drama includes the drama of the implicated 'boundary event' (Minh-ha, 2011).

Both the event of naming, and the event of the name, involve removing the anchor of 'proper' from the term 'proper name'.[3] The implications of this are huge and go to the heart of longstanding, contested debates about the proper name for distinctive, intersecting domains of feminism, and the name and position of 'differences that matter' (Ahmed, 1998) within feminism.

The dialectic of 'Black feminism' is in using the name to signify 'differences that matter' while contesting/resisting totalizing, homogenous, fixed domains that foreclose 'differences that matter'. Thinking specifically about the different domains of feminist scholarship – and, of course, this book concerns Black feminist scholarship – the words of Derrida present a set of interconnected challenges with wide-ranging ramifications for literary criticism:

> ... there is no such thing as a literary essence or a specifically literary domain strictly identifiable as such ... this name of literature perhaps is destined to remain improper, with no criteria, or assured concept or reference, so that "literature" has something to do with the drama of naming, the law of the name and the name of the law.
>
> (Derrida, 1992a: 187)

Perhaps Lorde recognized the essence of this in her creation of a biomythography, transgressing domains of the self (bio), writing (graphy) and myth genres. Thus, Lorde troubles the criteria for the domain of a conventional autobiography, which goes on to trouble the domains of prescribed identity and demarcations. This is illustrated in the 'Epilogue' of *Zami*, where the movement within self, myth and name is outside of, and precedes, given domains. Lorde explains that:

> *Ma-Liz, DeLois, Louise Briscoe, Aunt Anni, Linda, and Genevieve; MawuLisa, thunder, sky, sun, the great mother of us all; and Afrekete, her youngest daughter, the mischievous linguist, trickster, best-beloved, whom we must all become.* Their names, selves, faces feed me like corn before labor. I live each of them as a piece of me ...
>
> (Lorde, 1996: 223; italics in original)

Zami: A New Spelling of My Name is an interesting title and statement, since 'Zami' is neither a phonetic nor orthographic reconfiguration of the name 'Audre Lorde'.

Lorde's use of the name 'Zami' draws on the French expression, *les amies*, linking this to intimate connections between women so that the theme of Lorde's experience as a Black lesbian is performatively contained within the name of the text. This strategy challenges the notion of a determinate domain of text. *Zami* is simultaneously the title of the text and the subject of the text, the method for explicating messages within the text, and the signifier of Lorde's multiple subjectivities. Sánchez Calle comments that:

> The title of this book, *Zami: A New Spelling of My Name*, places it in the tradition of the slave narratives, in which slaves changed their names after reaching freedom. Likewise, Lorde, by choosing for herself a different name from the one her parents gave her, challenges the control of the dominant culture, and prevents others from speaking and naming on her behalf.
>
> (Sánchez Calle, 1996: 163; italics in original)

The politics of naming are picked up in Christian's (1990) analysis of how '[t]he name is made to do without the life of the bearer' (Derrida, 1987: 39) in relation to Black slave women writers. Christian provides a detailed account of the way that slave narratives were constructed to omit both the name and the life of the bearer. Christian cites the example of '*Incidents in the Life of a Slave Girl* (1861) written by Harriet Jacobs under the pseudonym, Linda Brent' (Christian, 1990: 222) and draws on Toni Morrison's introductory remarks to a public reading of *Beloved*, at which:

> Morrison pointed out that their omissions were partly due to the fact that these ex-slaves addressed a white audience. Even more important, she suggested, they omitted events too horrible and too dangerous for

them to recall. Morrison went on to state that these consistent comments made by nineteenth-century ex-slaves about the deliberate omissions in their narratives intrigued her and that this was the initial impulse for her writing the novel that would become *Beloved* ... in the last words of *Beloved*: "This was not a story to pass on."

(Christian, 1990: 222; italics in original)

These points are performatively embodied in Morrison's dedication of *Beloved* to the nameless '60 million or more' (Christian, 1990: 225).

duCille follows a similar analytic trajectory in her examination of the position of Black feminist writing:

One hundred thirty years ago, former slave Harriet Jacobs was able to publish her life's story only with the authenticating stamp of the well-known white abolitionist Lydia Maria Child as editor and copyright holder. "I have signed and sealed the contract with Thayer & Eldridge, in my name, and told them to take out the copyright in my name," Child wrote in a letter to Jacobs in 1860. "Under the circumstances *your* name could not be used, you know."

(duCille, 1994: 238; emphasis in original)

In a similar vein, Simmonds provides a contemporary context and incidence of appropriation of the name:

In public, at conferences for example, I insist that my full name appears on my name tag. In a society that cannot accommodate names that come from "other" cultures, this can be a frustrating exercise. It is no wonder that many Black children will Anglicize their names to avoid playground taunts ... and much worse. We are still fighting colonialism.

(Simmonds, 1996: 113; ellipsis in original)

The racist act of appropriating a name, documented here by duCille and Simmonds, is troubled by Derrida's distinction between the name and bearer of the name. Derrida explains that a name is '[a] property that one cannot appropriate; it signs you without belonging to you' (Derrida, n.d.: 119). The anxiety of the lacuna within the ambivalence of 'signs you without belonging to you', that is disavowed by the colonizer, is a potential space for subversion.

There is something freeing in the idea of the dead, unanchored name. While I appreciate the historical and political Black literary and Black vernacular traditions of the importance and use of names, Derrida's work offers the dialectic of the name as a site for anti-racist, anti-homophobic, feminist sedition. For example, contesting the property, signature and singularity of name, and deconstructing the 'proper' of 'proper name', function to contest and deconstruct oppressive constructions of authenticity. Derrida explains the aporia of the 'proper name' as:

> The proper name, in its aleatoriness, should have no meaning and should spend itself in immediate reference. But the chance or the misery of its arbitrary character (always other in each case) is that its inscription in language always affects it with a potential for meaning, and for no longer being proper once it has a meaning.
>
> (Derrida, 1984: 118)

Throughout this book, the aporia as a condition of thinking enables the possible within the impossible.

The significance of this in relation to the activism of Black feminist theory can be illustrated in the application of aporia as a condition to the components of the term 'Black feminist theory'. The aporia is an 'active' condition. The aporia messes up the condition of theory. The aporia messes up the condition of meanings inscribed in 'Black' and 'feminist'. I contend that the anarchy of aporia, the chaos, rebellion, lawlessness and mayhem of aporia provide conditions for feminist resistance and transformation.

Notes

1 See Ahmed (n.d.) and Mohr (2013) for examples of blogs.
2 Interestingly, the absence of a response from Daly to Lorde's letter prompted Lorde to write: 'The following letter was written to Mary Daly, author of Gyn/Ecology on May 6, 1979. Four months later, having received no reply, I opened it to the community of women' (Lorde, 1979c: 66).
3 The event is symbolized in the event/drama of naming ceremonies. In an interview with Dorothee Nolte, Lorde explains that '[i]n African cultures, the ritual bestowing of a name is of great significance ... A child receives its first name eight days after birth, but it receives new names at decisive events its whole life long' (Nolte, 1986: 143).

3 'Black feminism is not white feminism in blackface'

The question of Black-women-only[1] services and spaces

'Racist social structures create racist psychic structures' (Oliver, 2001: 34). A certain logic flows from this: we all live in a racist society; racism shapes our identity and makes us all racist subjects. Lorde and Fanon argue that this operates differently for Black and white people. Furthermore, Lorde and Fanon both argue that this has nothing and everything to do with the colour of skin. This chapter uses Lorde's statement that 'Black feminism is not white feminism in blackface' (Lorde, 1979b: 60) to anchor a critical analysis of why and how racist social structures operate differently for Black and white people. In other words, 'Black feminism is not white feminism in blackface' and could never be, precisely because 'racist social structures create racist psychic structures'. This chapter also uses this analysis to argue the case for Black-women-only service provision that takes account of the fact that racist social structures operate differently for Black women than they do for white women, white men and Black men.[2] Unfortunately, this logic becomes the basis for the following argument: because we are all constituted by racism, the specificity of being Black or white is redundant, or to highlight colour is to replicate racist structures, practices and thinking. It is a logic used to question the legitimacy of Black-women-only spaces. Lorde refers to this kind of logic in her statement: 'I can't tell you how many good white psychwomen have said to me, "Why should it matter if I am Black or white?" who would never think of saying, "Why does it matter if I am female or male?"' (Lorde, 1983a: 161–2).

Social structures create psychic structures

A close re-reading of Lorde's text and, in this case, of a sentence within Lorde's text, 'Black feminism is not white feminism in blackface', is used to demonstrate that the practice of close re-reading can be translated to the practice of critical psychology's challenge to the practice of psychology. In other words, the methodology used here moves between 'the deconstruction of texts and a more "practical" deconstruction of power relations, and the polarities that underlie and structure them' (Parker *et al.*, 1995: 131), thus provoking the question of 'who owns the definition of deconstruction?' (Parker *et al.*, 1995: 131). This question speaks to key themes of this book, which are the issues of ownership, belonging, inclusion and exclusion of the activism of theory. While the activism of Black feminist theory provokes the scrutiny of these themes, it is also subject to that same scrutiny. This is the dialectic that Caselli points to in saying that '[t]he metanarrative statement occupies an ambiguous position, as it is implicated in the narrative it criticises' (Caselli, 2005: 105). In order to demonstrate the wider implications and applications of tensions that feminism grapples with, this chapter moves between specific application to critical psychology and wider application to the activism of liberation theories in general, while picking up the particulars of the complexity of the debates that the activism of Black feminist theory raises for all feminisms.

An objective of this chapter is to use the example of the issue of Black-women-only services based on the specificity of Black women's position, representation, identity and experience to 'alert us to gaps in the growing orthodoxy of critical psychology' (Hook, 2005: n.p.). A Black feminist analysis of why 'Black feminism is not white feminism in blackface' is offered as an example of why critical psychology must position the activism of Black feminist theory at the heart of its work, in much the same way as feminism must position the activism of Black feminist theory at the heart of its work. In the context of critical psychology, 'Black feminism is not white feminism in blackface' could be restated as 'Black liberation psychology is not white liberation psychology in blackface' and, thus, the concepts are transferable to a diverse range of contexts. In other words, liberation ideological approaches, in order to be liberating at all, must take into consideration that particular social structures create particular psychic structures. An ideology does not become a Black ideology by painting a black face on it. A white, Eurocentric ideology or intervention does not convert to a Black version by having black faces in the literature, conferences, institutions or service provision. Any ideology, radical movement or force for social change does not become Black by increasing the representation of a particular pigmentation. So, it has nothing and everything to do with the colour of skin.

This analysis of Lorde's statement that 'Black feminism is not white feminism in blackface' argues that 'power that at first appears as external, pressed upon the subject, pressing the subject into subordination, assumes a psychic form that constitutes the subject's self-identity' (Butler, 1997a: 3), and this operates differently for Black women than for white women, white men and Black men. The question this provokes is: how does the 'psychic life of power' inhabit, and obtain agency through, the intersection of multiple axes of identity and power relations?

This chapter argues that racist, homophobic, patriarchal, subordinating power structures that appear as external get under the skin, into the psyche and go on to constitute Black women's self-identity in a way that is different than for white women, white men and Black men. Thus, the difference matters! Moreover, it is imperative that the differences that matter are taken into account, and the ways they are taken into account matter (Ahmed, 1998). The trouble is that Black women have, indeed, been treated as different within the psy-complex. There is a specificity to the psychologization of Black women based on the ideological position that: Black women require, for their own well-being, greater regulation and control; Black women's disorders are more deviant, abnormal and disordered than other people's, and this is why Black women are so unhappy and so unproductive; Black women do not have the personal resources required to enable them to sustain healthy relations, and are in need of the resources and treatments offered by psychology. In stark contrast to this, the activism of Black feminist theory insists on the specificity of Black women's difference as a tool of political resistance to confront oppressive ideologies, representations and structures that seek to regulate them.

The question of Black-women-only spaces

The necessity for Black-women-only service provision is legitimized within equality legislation,[3] demonstrated here in the judgement obtained by Southall Black Sisters in relation to domestic violence services. In the case of Kaur and Shah vs. London borough of Ealing 2008,[4] Lord Justice Moses clearly articulated the need for specialist services:

> There is no dichotomy between the promotion of equality and cohesion and the provision of specialist services to an ethnic minority. Barriers cannot be broken down unless the victims themselves recognise that the source of help is coming from the same community and background as they do. Ealing's mistake was to believe that cohesion and equality precluded the provision of services from such a source. It seemed to believe that such services could only lawfully be provided by a single provider or consortium to victims of domestic violence throughout the borough. It appreciates that it was in error and that in certain circumstances the purposes of Section 71 and the relevant statutory code may only be met by specialist services from a specialist source. That is the importance of the name of the Southall Black Sisters. Its very name evokes home and family.
>
> (Cited by Patel & Siddiqui, 2010: 121)

However, the issue of Black-women-only service provision is highly emotive, and even controversial. The questions – sometimes asked directly, sometimes indirectly, sometimes not asked, but it is obvious they are being thought and the thoughts hang in the air – are: why do you need to have specific services for Black women? Why have separate Black-women-only training, consciousness-raising and reflective spaces? What is so separate? What is so specific? The answers to these questions need careful scrutiny because the answers, and there are many answers, often fail to go to the heart of the issue and miss the point completely. The answers are difficult answers, not because they are too complicated; the answers are difficult because they are difficult to hear; they are uncomfortable. The answers hurt.

It is important to be clear about what is not the answer. The answer is not because of religion, culture, language, dress, geography, tradition or customs. The subordination, regulation and control of women and girls through physical, sexual, mental, financial and emotional abuse happen in every culture and use the same mechanisms the world over. It would seem, on the face of it, that there is a contradiction here: if the subordination and violation of women and girls use the same tools of regulation, control and legitimization, then why have specific support services for Black women? Why have Black-women-only spaces? What is so different?

Before examination of what the answer is, it is perhaps important to say what the answer is not. The wrong answers are particularly dangerous because they cover up and mask the real issues. The wrong answers function on camouflage and mimicry, so that when the real issues are voiced, when the real issues are made visible, they are not believed or recognized. What the answer is not is particularly dangerous because it silences Black women about the right answers. The result is that Black women are doubted and doubt themselves. Black women are silenced and keep silent. Black women know that the answers they are given are wrong. Black women know from their lived experience what the answer is not, and in the face of no alternatives, they feel confused, isolated, mad and bad. The result is that the wrong answers become translated into Black women being wrong. The wrong answers are camouflaged as psychopathology and this becomes the basis for treating the disordered psychology of Black women.

'Black feminism is not white feminism in blackface' is the opening sentence of Lorde's essay, 'Sexism: An American Disease in Blackface' (Lorde, 1979b: 60), first published in 1979 in the *Black Scholar* in response to *The Myth of Black Macho: A Response to Angry Black Feminists* by Staples (1979). Lorde critiques Staples' work, outlining the ways in which the intersection of sexism with racism operates to isolate Black women from others within their communities, resulting in deep trauma, lack of support and alienation. The statement that 'Black feminism is not white feminism in blackface' incorporates key themes, debates and issues central to the 'particular and legitimate issues which affect our lives as Black women' (Lorde, 1979b: 60). The point is that these are issues that are central to critical psychology and collective political mobilization of resistance to the racism of the psy-complex manifest in experiments, research, diagnostic categories, patient profiles and institutional cultures, politics, systems and practices. The challenge that the activism of Black feminist theory in general, and Lorde in particular, presents and needs to take account of is one of advocating the power of collective action while insisting on the recognition of difference.

Constitutive contexts

Detailed examination of what Lorde implies so concisely in her statement 'Black feminism is not white feminism in blackface' opens up rich layers of complexity that are at the core of feminist thinking, critical race theory, semiotics and literary criticism. This chapter insists that these are layers of complexity that are (or should be) at the core of the political critique that critical psychology levels at the production and function of the psy-complex. Lorde questions not only the definition, but also the related methodology and epistemology mobilized in the construction of difference and multiple identities. In her paper, 'Age, Race, Class and Sex: Women Redefining Difference', Lorde states that:

> Thus, in a patriarchal power system where whiteskin privilege is a major prop, the entrapments used to neutralize Black women and white women are not the same.
>
> (Lorde, 1980a: 118)

Here, Lorde is clear that the asymmetry between women is predicated upon the different ways that patriarchal power operates with regard to Black and white women. Pellegrini argues that:

> ... what starkly distinguishes "white" and "black" experiences of bodily self-consciousness, however, is their differential situation within the historico-psychical network of "race" ... the push-pull between "what is real and what is psychical" is all the more jarring for subjects who must embody and signify the borderlands of dominant frames of reference.
>
> (Pellegrini, 1997: 103)

Thus, Pellegrini points to the significance of context in the constitution of subjectivity and the processes of subjectification. Indeed, it will be apparent from this re-reading of 'Black feminism is not white feminism in blackface' that the context of the words within the statement itself reflects, and is performative of, the lived contexts in which the activism of 'theory as liberatory practice' (hooks, 1994: 59–75) is located. The key point is that contexts are constitutive. Pellegrini implies that the context of a racist, homophobic patriarchy is experienced by different women in different ways because of the signifiers 'Black' and 'white'. The implications of this in terms of the challenges made by critical psychology to the knowledge base and practice of psychology, and indeed, to all mental health service provision, including all practices and forms of intervention of well-being, are far reaching. It means that the notion of a 'one size fits all' approach in relation to ideologies, practices and forms of intervention will inevitably fail Black women. It also means that the basis for having specific service provision for Black women cannot simply rest on any quantitative, reductionist premise of numbers. Too often, the question (if it is considered at all) of whether a Black-women-only service is warranted is contingent upon whether there are sufficient numbers of Black, Asian and Minoritized Ethnic women within a geographical location.

Lorde demonstrates that the 'entrapments' (Lorde, 1980a: 118) in 'Black feminism is not white feminism in blackface' infer much more than a binary Black and/or white division. What is suggested by the statement is much more than a response to lack of inclusion of Black feminists on the part of white feminists, or indeed, that the development of Black-women-only service provision should be based on much more than a response to a lack of inclusion of Black women. Lorde is saying more than the fact that Black women are Other and Othered. Lorde is invoking an uncomfortable interdependency of difference, with the inherent political and epistemological problems, paradoxes and ambivalence of dependency and reliance on the Other, especially where there is a power differential. Butler interrogates the implications of interdependency in her statement that:

> ... when we think about who we "are" and seek to represent ourselves, we cannot represent ourselves as merely bounded beings, for the primary others who are past for me not only live on in the fibre of the boundary that contains me (one meaning of "incorporation"), but they also haunt the way I am, as it were, periodically undone and open to becoming unbounded.
>
> (Butler, 2004: 28; parentheses in original)

Butler's use of the words 'bounded', 'boundary' and 'unbounded', and Pellegrini's reference to 'borderlands of dominant frames of reference' (Pellegrini, 1997: 103), provide clues to suggest that the issues of borders and boundaries are fundamental to understanding the reasons why 'Black feminism is not white feminism in blackface'. Currie comments that 'the identity of things, people, places, groups, nations and cultures is constituted by the logics of both sameness and difference' (Currie, 2004: 3). The point here, in the context of 'Black feminism is not white feminism in blackface', is that the boundary of each word and the boundary of each category are contested. This dynamic is embodied and performed in the linguistic structure of the statement. Here, the Kristevan idea of intertextuality as intersubjectivity (Kristeva, 1969: 37) is crucial. Kristeva states that:

> ... each word (text) is an intersection of words (texts) where at least one other word (text) can be read ... any text is the absorption and transformation of another ... The word as minimal textual unit thus turns out to occupy the status of mediator, linking structural models to cultural (historical) environment, as well as that of *regulator*.
>
> (Kristeva, 1969: 37; parentheses and emphasis in original)

Thus, examination of the function, position, significance, constitution and configuration of the gap(s) between the words in 'Black feminism is not white feminism in blackface' is a method by which to deconstruct the intersubjective interdependence of the words. Recognition that the 'word is spatialized' (Kristeva, 1969: 37) has far-reaching implications. To be more specific, the space and place between the words in 'Black feminism is not white feminism in blackface' function as the space and place between Black and white subjects. In other words, intertexuality as intersubjectivity operates in an equation whereby the sum of the parts is greater than the individual elements, as in intersectionality.

Black without white?

'Black feminism is not white feminism in blackface' provokes questions such as: would there be Black feminism without white feminism? Can there be feminism without the prefixes of Black and white? Transposed onto the context of critical psychology or, indeed, any, activism of liberation theory, these questions provoke examination of how the signifiers 'Black' and 'white' function. In the short story *Recitatif* (1983), Morrison experimented with 'the removal of all racial codes from a narrative about two characters of different races for whom racial identity is crucial' (Morrison, 1992: xi). Seshadri-Crooks analyses *Recitatif* to ask: 'When the signifier "black" or "white" points to a specific body, what have we discovered about it? Is there some knowledge, something that we know, due to the function of the signifier?' (Seshadri-Crooks, 2000a: 148).

The problem is that of how to maintain the 'crucial' in relation to racial identity, which differentiates Black from white while wrestling with the

inherent paradoxes, ambivalence and interdependency. A particular difficulty lies in the process of identification. If the basis for identification is in
relation to the 'Other', and if for Black ideological approaches of emancipation the Other is white ideological approaches of emancipation, and vice-
versa, then both the relationality and the interdependency are paradoxical
on a cognitive level, but intensely uncomfortable on an emotional level.
Bhabha explains that:

> ... to be different from those that are different makes you the same – that
> the Unconscious speaks of the form of Otherness, the tethered shadow
> of deferral and displacement. It is not the Colonialist Self or the
> Colonized Other, but the disturbing distance in-between that constitutes
> the figure of colonial otherness ...
>
> (Bhabha, 1986, in Fanon, 2008: xxviii)

Tolerance: the grossest reformism

hooks' comment that 'it is unlikely that women would join feminist movement simply because we are biologically the same' (hooks, 1984: 24) opens
up the issues of ownership and identification, and questions the 'foundation
on which to construct theory or engage in overall meaningful praxis'
(hooks, 1984: 17). Both Lorde and hooks are pushing for a 'meaningful
praxis' that moves beyond 'the grossest reformism' of '[a]dvocating the
mere tolerance of difference' (Lorde, 1979b: 111). Lorde is suspicious of
the idea that '[t]he pronouncement "I am a tolerant man" conjures seemli-
ness, propriety, forbearance, magnanimity, cosmopolitanism, universality,
and the large view' (Brown, 2008: 178). It would appear that her suspicion
is well-founded. The Latin root of tolerance is 'tolero', derived from the
Greek verb 'talao', meaning 'to bear' and 'to endure', invoking a moral and
power differential that positions that which endures and that which has to
be endured. Brown (2008) picks up three particular angles presented in the
Oxford English Dictionary's definition:

> (1) "the action or practice of *enduring* pain or hardship"; (2) "the
> action of *allowing*; license, permission granted by an authority"; and
> (3) "the *disposition to be patient with or indulgent to* the opinions or
> practices of others ... "
>
> (Brown, 2008: 25; emphasis in original)

It would seem, then, that liberal discourses of 'tolerance' rest on constructions
that solidify, rather than dismantle, power differentials (DiBlasi & Holzhey,
2014). Brown's detailed examination of the function of tolerance argues that the

'Manichean rhetorical scheme' (Brown, 2008: 190) within the discourse and practice of tolerance to make the unknown known relies on a codification of differences into hierarchicalized binaries of "'fundamentalist/intolerant/unfree'" on the one side, and "'pluralist/tolerant/free" on the other' (Brown, 2008: 190). Application of this analysis of tolerance to 'Black feminism is not white feminism in blackface' signals a warning that any relationship between differences within theory as 'a location for healing' (hooks, 1994: 59) cannot rest on differences being tolerated. Any 'hierarchicalized opposites' (Brown, 2008: 189) of 'Black feminism is not white feminism' are disrupted by 'in blackface'. This disruption indicates that the task is so much more complicated than the binary of an either/or position of it 'is' and 'is not'. Brown's critical analysis of tolerance explains the complexity of how:

> Political and civic tolerance, then, emerges when a group difference that poses a challenge to the definitions or binding features of the whole must be incorporated but also must be sustained as a difference: regulated, managed, controlled.
>
> (Brown, 2008: 71)

'Black feminism is not white feminism in blackface' asserts Black feminism's refusal to be incorporated into white feminism, while asserting the specificity of difference in its own terms rather than any prescribed sustaining of difference.

The yardstick of fictive universality

Butler asks a number of related questions: 'Is there some commonality among "women" that pre-exists their oppression, or do "women" have a bond by virtue of their oppression alone?' (Butler, 2006: 5); 'Is the construction of the category of women as a coherent and stable subject an unwitting regulation and reification of gender relations? And is not such a reification precisely contrary to feminist aims?' (Butler, 2006: 7). Butler's use of the words 'commonality', 'bond', 'coherent', 'stable' and 'unwitting regulation and reification' question 'the shortcut to a categorical or fictive universality of the structure of domination, held to produce women's common subjugated experience' (Butler, 2006: 5). Lorde approaches the appeal of a 'fictive universality' in terms of:

> ... our refusal to recognize those differences, and to examine the distortions which result from our misnaming them and their effects upon human behavior and expectation. [...] Too often, we pour the energy needed for recognizing and exploring difference into pretending those

differences are insurmountable barriers, or that they do not exist at all. This results in a voluntary isolation, or false and treacherous connections.

(Lorde, 1980a: 115)

Both Butler and Lorde caution that the 'fictive', 'pretending', 'false' and 'misnaming' strategies of denial, exclusion and foreclosure are the requirements for a claim of universalism. The caution needs to be accompanied with the added caution of the dangers of using terms such as 'pretending', 'misnaming', 'false' and 'fictive' to propose, and thereby, fall into the trap of binary positions, the existence of a 'true', a 'real' and an 'authentic'. In her 1999 preface to *Gender Trouble*, Butler revises her understanding of:

> ... the claim of "universality" in exclusive negative and exclusionary terms
> [...] to understand how the assertion of universality can be proleptic and
> performative, conjuring a reality that does not yet exist, and holding out
> the possibility for a convergence of cultural horizons that have not yet met.
> (Butler, 1999: xviii)

The dialectic of 'conjuring a reality that does not yet exist' whilst being implicated in that which does exist is inferred in Lorde's statement that: 'Only within that interdependency of different strengths, acknowledged and equal, can the power to seek new ways of being in the world generate, as well as the courage and sustenance to act where there are no charters' (Lorde, 1979a: 111). This statement presents quite a challenge: change is contingent upon epistemology, which, according to Butler, 'does not yet exist' (Butler, 1999: xviii).

The challenge of the interdependency of difference is the task of grappling with the different entrapments used in the 'psychic life of power' (Butler, 1997a) to neutralize Black and white women without 'charters'. Mohanty's (1984) paper, 'Under Western Eyes: Feminist Scholarship and Colonial Discourses', addresses the strategies, mechanisms and structures in which:

> ... the application of the notion of women as a homogeneous category
> to women in the Third World colonizes and appropriates the pluralities
> of the simultaneous location of different groups of women in social
> class and ethnic frameworks; in doing so it ultimately robs them of
> their historical and political agency.
> (Mohanty, 1984: 39)

Mohanty goes on to add:

> In other words, Western feminist discourse, by assuming women as a
> coherent, already constituted group that is placed in kinship, legal, and

other structures, defines Third World women as subjects outside social relations, instead of looking at the way women are constituted through these very structures.

(Mohanty, 1984: 40)

Mohanty is saying that the assumption that Black women are a stable, 'coherent' group is a construction produced out of a particular set of conditions and power relations that must be taken account of. Spivak (1988) adds further layers of complexity: 'Between patriarchy and imperialism, subject-constitution and object-formation, the figure of the woman disappears, not into a pristine nothingness, but into a violent shuttling which is the displaced figuration of the "third-world woman" caught between tradition and modernization' (Spivak, 1988: 306).

Both Mohanty and Spivak are highlighting the specificity of the entrapments used to neutralize Black women, and indicate that ideology produces Black women as an 'already constituted group' (Mohanty, 1984: 40). The 'already' operates through the 'sly civility' (Bhabha, 1994: 93) of these entrapments to foreclose and constrain critical analysis. Mohanty reflects that:

... I am trying to uncover how ethnocentric universalism is produced in certain analyses. As a matter of fact, my argument holds for any discourse that sets up its own authorial subjects as the implicit referent, that is, the yardstick by which to encode and represent cultural others. It is in this move that power is exercised in discourse.

(Mohanty, 1984: 21)

The challenge for all theories and practices of liberation, including the activism of Black feminist theory, lies in resistance to being seduced into replicating the 'authorial subjects', 'implicit referent' and 'yardstick' (Mohanty, 1984: 21) embodied in the 'claim to authenticity' (Suleri, 1992: 251). The tension is in the stating of a position in order to undo a position.

'Black feminism is not white feminism in blackface' goes to the heart of fundamental questions concerning the basis, membership, definition and objectives of all theories and practices of liberation. The statement provokes questions of: who and what is foreclosed? Who is constituted, in what ways and why? Butler asks:

What kinds of agency are foreclosed through the positing of an epistemological subject precisely because the rules and practices that govern the invocation of that subject and regulate its agency in advance are ruled out as sites of analysis and critical intervention?

(Butler, 2006: 197)

Butler exposes the temporal trick of the 'in advance' that functions to rule out subversive ideas. In other words, and to pick up on the point made earlier, the impetus to examine an 'already constituted group' (Mohanty, 1984: 40) may be less than the impetus to examine that which is new and unfamiliar. In transgressing the 'already' and in destabilizing the 'in advance', Lorde's statement that 'Black feminism is not white feminism in blackface' embodies and performs its own deconstruction. Butler explains this dynamic in the following way: 'The deconstruction of identity is not the deconstruction of politics; rather, it establishes as political the very terms through which identity is articulated' (Butler, 2006: 203). Therefore, 'Black feminism is not white feminism in blackface' 'establishes as political the very terms through which' the activism of Black feminism is articulated and identified.

In thinking about the 'sites of analysis and critical intervention' that 'are ruled out' (Butler, 2006: 197), for Bacchi, the primary issue is not one of sameness or difference, but:

> ... the question becomes: why has this "difference" been constructed as disadvantage? If women are in fact the "same", the problem of their relative disadvantage and lack of power remains unresolved. There is a need therefore to shift the focus of analysis from the "difference" to the structures which convert this "difference" into disadvantage.
>
> (Bacchi, 1990: xviii, cited in Currie, 2004: 88)

Juxtaposing Butler's and Bacchi's lines of inquiry, it could be argued that the positing of epistemology of women as the 'same' forecloses the play of unequal power differentials. This happens because the 'structures', 'rules and practices' that 'govern', 'convert' and 'regulate' 'difference into disadvantage' are ruled out. Critical intervention would include a shift in vision to realise a new charter and 'convergence of cultural horizons' (Butter, 1999: xviii), asking different questions and re-working the primary issue of sameness and difference.

Injurious interpellations

Althusser explains that:

> ... ideology "acts" or "functions" in such a way that it "recruits" subjects among the individuals (it recruits them all), or "transforms" the individuals into subjects (it transforms them all) by that very precise operation which I have called *interpellation* or hailing, and which can be imagined along the lines of the most commonplace everyday police (or other) hailing: "Hey, you there!"
>
> (Althusser, 1971: 33; parentheses and emphasis in original)

It is precisely because 'the space and place we inhabit produce us' (Probyn, 2003: 294) that the recruitment is different for different individuals, and the transforming is different for different individuals. Black ideology is not white ideology in blackface because 'we are interpellated differently' and 'we are hailed by different ideologies in different ways' (Probyn, 2003: 298). So, the Black and white psyche are constituted and regulated differently because they occupy different spaces, and are recruited and transformed differently.

Even if one were to argue that the oppressive effects of the psy-complex are universal, liberation ideologies cannot be universally applied because we are hailed and constituted as subjects differently. In *The Psychic Life of Power*, Butler speaks of a 'passionate attachment' to 'injurious interpellations' (Butler, 1997a: 7 and 104, respectively). So, there is the hailing and there is the 'passionate attachment' to the hailing, even when the hailing is oppressive. Because Black people are recruited, transformed and attached differently than white people, and white people are recruited, transformed and attached differently than Black people, the ideology required to look at the specificity of the recruitment, the specificity of the transformation and the specificity of the attachment cannot be the same for Black and white people. Here, the issue of recognition and misrecognition is fundamental (Ahmed, 1998: 114; 2000: 23–4). What is recognized or not recognized determines whether or not 'we lose sight of the complex and multiple ways' (Alarcón, 1990: 361) in which different subjects are hailed and constituted. The inquiry and activism of theory as liberatory practice (hooks, 1994: 59–75) must examine the detail of the 180-degree turning as an act in direct response to a hailing that recognizes subjects differently (for example, on the basis of skin colour and gender), and, in turn, is recognized differently by different subjects (for example, recognition operates differently for Black women in relation to white women, white men and Black men).

The ideologies propagated within a racist, homophobic patriarchy hail and recognize Black and white subjects differently. The specific mechanisms used in the interpellation of Black subjectivity are explored by a range of Black feminist scholars (Amos & Parmar, 1984; Davis, 1981; hooks, 1982; Mirza, 1997). Keizer's (2004) use of Althusser's theory of interpellation to interpret Morrison's (1987) *Beloved* is a good example of this particular line of inquiry. Keizer examines Morrison's 'explicit concern with the mechanisms – coercive and consensual – that slaveholders used to construct and control black men and women call to mind Louis Althusser's theory of interpellation' (Keizer, 2004: 13).

Taking up these issues in 'An Open Letter to Mary Daly', Lorde speaks frankly and with powerful directness:

To imply, however, that all women suffer the same oppression simply because we are women is to lose sight of the many and varied tools of patriarchy. It is to ignore how these tools are used by women without awareness against each other.

(Lorde, 1979c: 67)

In the same letter, Lorde concludes that 'beyond sisterhood is still racism' (Lorde, 1979c: 70). The inherent tension is that political activism is constituted by the very conditions it seeks to resist and, as such, the challenge is how to mitigate replication of these conditions. Lorde's use of the word 'tools' is crucial because if the 'many varied tools' of a racist, homophobic patriarchy are not both identified and resisted, the danger is that these tools become unwittingly stitched into the fabric of the work of, and relationships between, political activists. The tools used to fight oppression need to be sharp, precise and fit for the job. Perhaps it is useful, therefore, to think about a mechanics of theory in order to encourage a labouring on the engineering of theory. Furthermore, the subjects under analysis (for example, the concepts, issues and tensions that require engineering) constitute the tools required for the job. In other words, 'Black feminism is not white feminism in blackface' is at once the subject under analysis and constitutes the tools for analysis. 'Beyond sisterhood', indeed beyond Black-women-only service provision and spaces, there is still racism, and this applies whether a woman self-defines as a Black or white feminist.

The issue at the heart of 'Black feminism is not white feminism in blackface' that concerns all theories and practices of emancipation is whether there can be a political activism of liberation theory that doesn't replicate, or become, a simple inversion of binary divisions, tolerance, regulation and reification. Thieme's caution about the potential effect of post-colonial theory functioning as a 'straitjacket', shackle or an occlusion is applicable here:

> ... the term "postcolonial", which initially promised liberation from some of the hegemonic assumptions of the Western academy, has itself threatened to become a straitjacket, shackling or occluding the differences that exist amid the particular creative energies of the many peoples, places and agendas it has subsumed into its project.

(Thieme, 2001: 6)

The 'not'

'Black feminism is not white feminism in blackface' is not simply referring to sameness and difference. Lorde not only troubles the notion of a shared feminism, but she also introduces the 'not'. In 'Black feminism is not', the distinction between Black feminism and white feminism is made available by the 'not'. This should not be confused with fixed, oppositional, essentialist categories of Black and white. Brah explains that:

... they are fields of contestation inscribed within discursive and material processes and practices in a post-colonial terrain. They represent struggles over political frameworks for analysis; the meanings of theoretical concepts; the relationship between theory, practice and subjective experiences, and over political priorities and modes of mobilisation. But they should not, in my view, be understood as constructing "white" and "black" women as "essentially" fixed oppositional categories.

(Brah, 1996: 110)

People inhabit different physical, geographical, social, economic, emotional and ideological spaces and places, and, therefore, it follows that different subjective experiences will be produced. Service provision, practices and the knowledge that underpins these are products of space and place, and, as such, they must take account of the physical, geographical, social, economic, emotional and ideological spaces and places they seek to intervene in. Indeed, location mediates and produces meaning, and becomes a site of either appropriation or resistance.

Both the spaces between the words in 'Black feminism is not white feminism in blackface' and the relation of one word to the other are performative of the relationality of intersubjectivity. The configuration of the words is representative of the configuration of the Black subject in relation to the white subject. The 'not' is only the 'not' in relation to what it actually is, or the opposite of 'not'. The claim of what Black feminism 'is not' is contingent upon a notion of what Black feminism 'is'. There are several intersecting tensions here: the 'not' is only the 'not' in relation to what it actually is, or is not, and this is highly problematic because it edges far too close to the dangerous claim of an authentic subject. The danger here is that of predicating the 'not' on a claim of authenticity. However, a close re-reading of the use of the 'not' in 'Black feminism is not white feminism in blackface' appears to invoke an authenticity of Black feminism. This could be an example of an intervention of the '*strategic* use of positivist essentialism' (Spivak, 2006: 281; emphasis in original) in order to guard against misrecognition of 'white feminism in blackface'. Black can only be Black because it is not white, and white is white because it is not Black; thus, Black and white are mutually constitutive. The border between Black and white produces a false binary. The predicament is that the 'not' demarcates the border of specificity that enables us to distinguish Black feminism from white feminism – how else could we spot the masquerade of white feminism in 'blackface'? However, borders are indeterminable; borders are mutually constitutive; the tension is that borders are not real, they are constructions that cease to exist under deconstruction (Thiongo, 1996: 120).

The challenge for Black feminism lies in the problematic of establishing coherence, and a sense of what Black feminism stands for when all representations are unstable and relational, while keeping hold of the political imperative of suspecting a masquerade or misrecognition. Returning to the concern raised at the beginning of this chapter regarding answers to the questions about why there is a necessity for Black-women-only services, it would appear that the wrong answer, or what the answer is *not*, is constituted by what it excludes and leaves outside – namely, what the answer *is*: and this is a clear example of the 'constitutive outside' (Hall, 1996: 17) in operation. The quandary is that of how to create Black-women-only spaces and services that give voice to the specificity of particular entrapments while also giving voice to the interdependency of difference, without falling foul of authenticity and borders.

To summarize, 'racist social structures create racist psychic structures' (Oliver, 2001: 34) even though the recruitment, transformation and 'passionate attachment' (Butler, 1997a: 7) are different, and the 'not' reminds us that the difference is in relation to, interdependent on, and contingent upon, the 'not'.

The problem of the 'native informant'

Mohanty adds further complexity to the debate, stating that:

> If relations of domination and exploitation are defined in terms of binary divisions – groups that dominate and groups that are dominated – then surely the implication is that the accession to power of women as a group is sufficient to dismantle the existing organization of relations. But women as a group are not in some sense essentially superior or infallible. The crux of the problem lies in that initial assumption of women as a homogeneous group …
>
> (Mohanty, 1984: 39)

The premise that unequal gender relations bind women together in a shared discourse, and the assumption that women are a homogeneous group, are contested. However, the temptation to form factions and impose a ranking of whose difference or whose group is more or less oppressed (Lorde, 1983b: 219–20) function to replicate existing power relations and result in 'a simple inversion of what exists' (Mohanty, 1984: 39). Bhabha (1994) poses a number of relevant questions:

> Must we always polarize in order to polemicize? Are we trapped in a politics of struggle where the representation of social antagonisms and

historical contradictions can take no other form than a binarism of theory vs politics? Can the aim of freedom of knowledge be the simple inversion of the relation of oppressor and oppressed, centre and periphery, negative image and positive image?

(Bhabha, 1994: 19)

hooks (1984) makes several points that are pertinent to this discussion. hooks names and exposes strategies used to flatten out epistemology (Alarcón, 1990: 361), and used to posit the 'already constituted' epistemological subject of Black women:

> ... the slogan "the personal is political" ... became a means of encouraging women to think that the experience of discrimination, exploitation, or oppression automatically corresponded with an understanding of the ideological and institutional apparatus shaping one's social status [...] When women internalized the idea that describing their own woe was synonymous with developing a critical political consciousness, the progress of feminist movement was stalled.
>
> (hooks, 1984: 24–5)

hooks argues that an aspect of the stalling serves to re-inscribe the 'hegemonic dominance of white academic women' (hooks, 1984: 30) and privileges the claim of giving voice to Black, poor, marginalized women at the expense of creating an inclusive developing theory. The consequences of this include the invocation of marginalized women in any liberatory approach, including critical psychology, on the basis of their '"experiential" work, personal life stories' (hooks, 1984: 30). hooks concludes that 'Personal experiences are important ... but they cannot take the place of theory' (hooks, 1984: 30). The issue that hooks is flagging up here is that to position experience in the place of theory serves to freeze the Black subject into a fixed, essentialist position. This serves as a basis for an authenticity that, by definition, is divorced from the tools of critical analysis.

Spivak's reference to the problem of the 'Native Informant' as 'truth' resonates with hooks' critique of feminism:

> If one looks at the history of post-Enlightenment theory, the major problem has been the problem of autobiography: how subjective structures can, in fact, give objective truth. During these same centuries, the Native Informant ... was unquestioningly treated as the objective evidence for the founding of so called sciences ... So that, once again, the theoretical problems only relate to the person who knows. The person

who *knows* has all of the problems of selfhood. The person who is *known*, somehow seems not to have a problematic self.

(Spivak, 1986: 66; emphasis in original)

Thus, the use of autobiographical foundations for 'knowing' is beset with problems, not least that of positing an epistemological subject on the basis of privileging claims of a decided personhood. The relevance of these points to 'Black feminism is not white feminism in blackface' is that Lorde is both positing and troubling a *knowing* of what it means to be Black. She straddles the dialectic of positing that the selfhood of race is relational whilst functioning to maintain differences.

The constitutive interstices of feminisms

The importance of process in the dialectic articulated above is emphasized by Bhabha: 'What is theoretically innovative, and politically crucial, is the need to think beyond narratives of originary and initial subjectivities and to focus on those moments or processes that are produced in the articulation of cultural differences' (Bhabha, 1994: 1). Here, Bhabha contests the very existence of an 'originary and initial' subjectivity as part of the dialectic of difference. He proposes that energy should not be directed towards the location of 'originary and initial subjectivities' but, rather, towards dismantling process and production. For Bhabha, theoretical engagement requires 'the emergence of the interstices – the overlap and displacement of domains of difference' (Bhabha, 1994: 2).

The configuration of 'Black feminism is not white feminism in blackface' directs attention to the interstices that constitute different 'isms'. Lorde is indicating that there is a space between Black and white feminisms, and that the space matters. The issue for the activism of 'theory as liberatory practice' (hooks, 1994: 59–75) is that of what happens to the 'personal experiences' and 'personal life stories' that hooks (1984: 30) refers to within Bhabha's (1994: 2) inevitable interstices.

This is further complicated by the notion of Black women as migratory subjects who occupy 'that in-between space that is neither here nor there' (Boyce Davies, 1994: 1). However, rather than intervening to fix Black feminism in the 'in-between space' (an intervention used for the purposes of taking hold of, and appropriating, Black feminism), all emancipatory approaches need to 'activate the term "Black" relationally, provisionally and based on location or position' (Boyce Davies, 1994: 8). It could be argued that the construction and use of the statement 'Black feminism is not white feminism in blackface' anticipates many of the arguments found in post-modernist, deconstructionist theory concerning positionality, relationality and contestations of an originary. Boyce Davies makes this point in relation to Black feminist scholarship in general:

> My contention is that postmodernist positions or feminist positions are always already articulated by Black women because we experience, ahead of the general population, many of the multiple struggles that subsequently become popularly expressed (for example, drugs in communities, teen pregnancies, struggle for control of one's body, one's labor, etc.). Black feminist criticisms, then, perhaps more than many of the other feminisms, can be a praxis where the theoretical positions and the criticism interact with the lived experience.
>
> (Boyce Davies, 1994: 55)

The subject of experience emerges again here. However, Boyce Davies offers an example of using experience not to displace, but to interact with theory, thereby using experience as a vital element in the process of formulating theory, rather than positioning experience in the place of theory. It could be argued that 'Black feminism is not white feminism in blackface' because of the interaction of experience with theory. The experiences of Black women are different to the experiences of white women in the context of a racist, homophobic patriarchy. Throughout *Sister Outsider* (1984), Lorde continually addresses the issue of how to think about the position, and positioning, of intersubjectivity without inverting existing power relations.

In the following quotation, Lorde questions the 'terms of oppression' that constitute the 'ticket' to move from the position of being 'outside' to 'inside' the 'fold':

> What woman here is so enamoured of her own oppression that she cannot see her heelprint upon another woman's face? What woman's terms of oppression have become precious and necessary to her as a ticket into the fold of the righteous, away from the cold winds of self-scrutiny?
>
> (Lorde, 1981: 132)

A close re-reading of Lorde's words in conjunction with Butler's (1997a) analysis of *The Psychic Life of Power* enables a nuanced exploration of the mechanisms and impetus that Lorde is referring to. In answer to the question of 'What woman's terms of oppression have become precious and necessary to her...?' (Lorde, 1981: 132), Butler might respond:

> Called by an injurious name, I come into social being, and because I have certain inevitable attachment to my existence, because a certain

narcissism takes hold of any term that confers existence, I am led to embrace the terms that injure me because they constitute me socially.

(Butler, 1997a: 104)

Both Lorde and Butler take up the idea of damage and harm conjured in the reference to 'injury' and the image of the 'heelprint'. Indeed, Butler speaks of 'those injurious interpellations' (Butler, 1997a: 104). Lorde and Butler make similar claims: the 'narcissism' of being 'so enamoured by her own oppression' as to 'embrace the terms that injure me' is fuelled by the impulse or desire to 'embrace' and to become 'so enamoured' as to 'take hold of any term', 'precious and necessary'.

Bringing in the components of desire and attachment underscores the need for rigorous vigilance on the part of Black and white political activists in order to resist insidious, oppressive forces of stability, inclusion and acceptance in the face of racist, homophobic, patriarchal rejections and exclusions. Butler explains that 'the attachment to subjection is produced through the workings of power, and that part of the operation of power is made clear in this psychic effect, one of the most insidious of its productions' (Butler, 1997a: 6). Ahmed also takes up the question of the function and relationship of attachment to power: 'how do such attachments to feminism relate to attachments that already exist in the everyday world, including those that are bound up with the reproduction of the very forms of power that feminism seeks to contest[?]' (Ahmed, 2004: 171). In relation to the 'terms' Lorde refers to in the passage quoted earlier, she is identifying the insidious, plausible binary positions of precious/not precious, necessary/unnecessary, righteous/unrighteous that will, ultimately, result in Mohanty's 'inversion of what exists' (Mohanty, 1984: 39).

The performative regime of visibility

'Black feminism is not white feminism in blackface' invokes the performative regime of visibility. Seshadri-Crooks' (2000a) detailed examination of the function and meaning of visibility, the looking and seeing in racism, underscores the significance of Lorde's uses of 'Black' and 'white'. Seshadri-Crooks clarifies her theoretical approach:

> Thus by visibility I refer to a regime of looking that thrives on "major" and "minor" details in order to shore up one's symbolic position ... I therefore focus on race as a practice of visibility ... My premise is that the regime of visibility secures the investment that we make in "race," and there are good reasons why such an investment cannot be easily surrendered.
>
> (Seshadri-Crooks, 2000a: 2)

'Black feminism is not white feminism in blackface' invokes a relationship between the regime of visibility, and that which is included and excluded. Thus, in the statement 'Black feminism is not white feminism in blackface', the word 'feminism' is a potential – although contested – site of inclusion, but being 'Black' or 'white' is a potential site of exclusion. This complex relationship of difference is examined by Seshadri-Crooks, who claims that '[r]ace is fundamentally a regime of looking' (Seshadri-Crooks, 2000a: 2) and that:

> By Whiteness, I refer to a master signifier (without a signified) that establishes a structure of relations, a signifying chain that through a process of inclusions and exclusions constitutes a pattern for organizing human difference. This chain provides subjects with certain symbolic positions such as "black," "white," ... We will therefore have to see how this symbolic structuration is related to visibility.
>
> (Seshadri-Crooks, 2000a: 3–4; parentheses in original)

In 'What's in a name?...' (2000a), Seshadri-Crooks uses Butler's deconstruction of gender as a category of representation, identity and identification to interrogate:

> What does it mean to point with the noun "black" or "white" ... What kind of words are these? Do they possess a meaning, or connote a concept, that remains identical with itself in all situations, or do their predicates determine the meaning of these words, thus making subject and predicate synonymous with each other? Is there any "sense" to naming someone black or white?
>
> (Seshadri-Crooks, 2000a: 137)

These questions and, indeed, the whole of Seshadri-Crooks' chapter, 'What's in a name?...' are relevant because of the critical examinations of gender, race and performativity, and deceptions of coherence, unity and stability in identity categories. Furthermore, Seshadri-Crooks' (2000a) analysis provides a critical, theoretical microscope to scrutinize the categories of 'Black' and 'white'. Seshadri-Crooks articulates the complexity of the task that could be applied not only to this particular, close re-reading of Lorde's statement, but to the activism of all liberation theories:

> If one begins from the perspective of power as the ultimate productive force in the construction of categories – binary, monologic or differential – then one's task is usually focussed on exposing the sandy bottom of power's foundational pretensions. One's critical task, to put

it rather reductively, is to eliminate the modality of necessity and install in its place the contingency of all relations.

(Seshadri-Crooks, 2000a: 136)

'Blackface'

Of all the different premises available to distinguish Black feminism from white feminism, Lorde rests her case on 'blackface' and, as such, draws on, and opens up, a range of images, connotations and inferences. This chapter follows up on the inference to mimicry invoked in the word 'blackface'. The activism of Black feminist theory warns against the mimicry of inversion, the 'false and treacherous connections' (Lorde, 1980a: 115) of fictive feminist universalities, and the unwitting regulation and reification of epistemology based solely on gender.

Lorde's gaze on 'blackface' plays with the shifting, contradictory, racist genre of minstrelsy. Blackface minstrelsy used slapstick, stump speech and romanticized and exaggerated stereotypes. These strategies can be seen in the Black slave, caricatured by the following figures: Jim Crow; the Black servant; the mammy; the dandy, represented by Zip Coon; and the mulatto wench, who personified the exoticized sexual promiscuity of Black women embodied in light-skinned, Caucasian features (Toll, 1974). Lott's study of the social and psychological function of blackface minstrelsy illustrates that the acting out of the grotesque, animalistic, infantilization of Black people provided a vehicle for the projective identifications of white audiences (Lott, 1993: 143–8). The performative juxtaposition of figures such as Tambo and Mr Bones reiterated racist power dynamics. The dynamics of embodied simple-mindedness in the ersatz form of Black vernacular English, with the blackface interlocutor representative of educated sophistication in the voice of aristocratic English, functioned to heighten and re-inscribe unequal power differentials. The performance also encompassed the paradox of the 'conflictual economy of colonial discourse' (Bhabha, 1994: 85). Lorde's reference to 'blackface' provocatively invokes and conflates the conscious and unconscious associations of Black and white signifiers mediated through genres such as Black minstrelsy, simultaneously conjuring Bhabha's mimicry, sly civility and hybridity of 'the "not quite/not white"' (Bhabha, 1994: 92).

Mimicry

Bhabha defines mimicry as 'the desire for a reformed, recognizable Other, *as a subject of a difference that is almost the same, but not quite*' (Bhabha, 1994: 86; emphasis in original). It is in the 'area between mimicry and mockery' (Bhabha, 1994: 86) or in the 'not' in 'Black feminism is not white feminism in blackface' that 'mimicry is constructed around an *ambivalence*; in order to be effective, mimicry must continually produce its slippage, its excess, its difference' (Bhabha, 1994: 86; emphasis in original). In other words, in the context of colonization, any form of white feminism in 'blackface' would be an example of colonization. The colonizer constructs the colonized as *'almost the same, but not quite'* because the success of the takeover rests on maintaining the difference between the colonized and the colonizer; the colonizer cannot afford the colonized to make the mistake of thinking that they are equal. Well, this is a stressful situation.

The 'not in blackface' in 'Black feminism is not white feminism in blackface', or, in Bhabha's words, the 'irony of partial representation' points to the 'menace', 'strategic limitation or prohibition' or 'metonymy of presence' (Bhabha, 1994: 85–92). Aligning Seshadri-Crooks, Butler, Lorde and Bhabha with a focus on how the 'not' operates amplifies the performative 'repetition of partial presence' that 'rearticulates presence in terms of otherness', so that 'Mimicry *repeats* rather than *re-presents*' (Bhabha, 1994: 88; emphasis in original).

Throughout *Sister Outsider*, Lorde examines the colonization of the psychic space through the mechanism of mimicry. She incorporates aspects of Bhabha's explanation that:

> In mimicry, the representation of identity and meaning is rearticulated along the axis of metonymy. As Lacan reminds us, mimicry is like camouflage, not a harmonization of repression of difference, but a form of resemblance, that differs from or defends presence by displaying it in part, metonymically.
>
> (Bhabha, 1994: 90)

Lorde uses metonymy performatively to conjure in the reader's imagination the ways that mimicry operates in the 'psychic life of power'. Lorde repeatedly cautions against masquerades of emancipatory transformation, and the following passages provide examples of how she picks up this theme throughout *Sister Outsider*:

> The old patterns, no matter how cleverly rearranged to imitate progress, still condemn us to cosmetically altered repetitions of the same old exchanges, the same old guilt, hatred, recrimination, lamentation, and suspicion.
>
> (Lorde, 1980a: 123)

> And when I speak of change, I do not mean a simple switch of positions ...
>
> (Lorde, 1981: 127)

My poetry, my life, my work, my energies for struggle were not acceptable unless I pretended to match somebody else's norm. I learned that not
only couldn't I succeed at that game, but the energy needed for that
masquerade would be lost to my work.

(Lorde, 1982: 137)

But if the quest to reclaim ourselves and each other remains there, then
we risk another superficial measurement of self, one superimposed upon
the old one and almost as damaging, since it pauses at the superficial.

(Lorde, 1983a: 174)

Evidently, mimicry operates not only to appropriate, but also to stall
progress. Drawing threads of the discussion together concerning configuration, disavowal, entrapments, implicit referents, location and regulation
suggests that the metonym 'blackface' stands for an inextricable web of
constructions that configure particular, precarious relations of proximity.
Relations between Black and white feminism are contingent upon 'injurious
interpellations' (Butler, 1997a: 104), predicated on the regime of visibility.
Post-colonial theory offers an analogous lens to scrutinize the mechanisms
and manoeuvres of the 'psychic life of power', which are relevant to the
activism of all liberation theories.

Picking up references used earlier in this chapter in relation to how 'epistemology is flattened' (Alarcón, 1990: 361), the 'authorial subjects as the
implicit referent' (Mohanty, 1984: 21) and Lorde's (1979c: 66–71) letter to
Mary Daly, it is clear that the role of epistemology is not merely academic.
Butler pulls together the relationship between the structure and constitution
of address, and interdependency of difference:

The structure of address is important for understanding how moral
authority is introduced and sustained if we accept not just that we
address others when we speak, but that in some way we come to exist,
as it were, in the moment of being addressed, and something about our
existence proves precarious when that address fails.

(Butler, 2004: 130)

Here, Butler explains the paradox of adopting a speaking position and being
simultaneously undone by that position, and the same could be applied to
all forms of representing and communicating epistemology. The tension is
one of making a coherent, assertive, persuasive, political address as
evidence of existence, while knowing that the inevitable failure of the
address reflects something of the precarity of existence. This situation is
acutely amplified in relation to Black and white feminisms because it

provokes questions about how they listen and address each other, and what is at stake.

Do the manners of Black feminists need reforming?

Staying with the tactic of mimicry, the parallels between the doctrine of Christianity and bureaucracy as imperial devices of regulatory colonial power, with the regulatory aspects of the doctrine of feminism, can be detected. Bhabha (1994) details numerous examples of how bureaucracy, in many different guises, functions as an instrument of regulation. Bhabha states that Charles Grant's:

> ... dream of an evangelical system of mission education conducted uncompromisingly in the English language, was partly a belief in political reform along Christian lines and partly an awareness that the expansion of company rule in India required a system of subject formation – a reform of manners ...
>
> (Bhabha, 1994: 87)

Perhaps, here, the question for the 'dream' of feminism concerns not only the language used, but what the deployment of that language functions to do. The following questions make this point in concrete terms: is the language used by feminism for the reform of manners, and, if so, whose manners and what particular manners require reforming? If feminism is a movement for the emancipation of all women, then is there some notion that the manners of non-academic women need reforming into the ways of those women in academia? Do the manners of Black feminists need reforming? Bhabha refers to Sir Edward Cust's 'policy of a conferring on every colony of the British Empire a mimic representation of the British Constitution' (Cust, 1839, cited in Bhabha, 1994: 85). Bhabha also refers to J.S. Mill's testimony to a Select Committee of the House of Lords in 1852, and quotes that: "'The whole government of India is carried out in writing," ... This appears to me a greater security for good government than exists in almost any other government in the world, because no other has a system of recordation so complete' (Mill, 1852, cited in Bhabha, 1994: 93).

Perhaps in relation to the security of feminism, the issue could be articulated in terms of a critical analysis of the production and function of feminist archives and records. Furthermore, the issue is that of what is included and excluded in feminist records, and who the stakeholders are. Referring to feminist scholarship, Mohanty cautions of 'a certain mode of appropriation and codification of scholarship' (Mohanty, 1984: 17) Bhabha is clear that the examples he examines demonstrate an effort to 'construct a particularly appropriate form of colonial subjectivity' (Bhabha, 1994: 87). However, the result is only 'partial reform' (Bhabha, 1994: 87). Spivak fittingly names the practice 'epistemic violence' (Spivak, 1988: 280).

Spivak's deconstruction of ideology as a tool of appropriation is clear in her seminal work, 'Can the Subaltern Speak?'(1988). Here, Spivak challenges the intellectual equivalents of the British Constitution and Christian doctrine in her challenge of Foucault, Deleuze and Marx. Spivak considers:

> ... a text by two great practitioners of the critique: "Intellectuals and Power: A Conversation between Michel Foucault and Gilles Deleuze" ... because it undoes the opposition between authoritative theoretical production and the unguarded practice of conversation, enabling one to glimpse the track of ideology.
>
> (Spivak, 1988: 272)

Spivak argues that the track of ideology demonstrates that 'Western intellectual production is, in many ways, complicit with Western international economic interests' (Spivak, 1988: 271). In relation to 'Black feminism is not white feminism in blackface', the key point would be to consider the intellectual production of feminism within the context of prevailing socio-economic conditions and interests. Making the parallel between imperial devices of regulation and intellectual production explicit, Spivak observes that:

> Sometimes it seems as if the very brilliance of Foucault's analysis of the centuries of European imperialism produces a miniature version of that heterogeneous phenomenon: management of space – but by doctors; development of administrations – but in asylums; considerations of the periphery – but in terms of the insane, prisoners, and children. The clinic, the asylum, the prison, the university – all seem to be screen-allegories that foreclose a reading of the broader narratives of imperialism.
>
> (Spivak, 1988: 291)

The interdictory discourse embodied in 'Black feminism is not white feminism in blackface' encapsulates the relationality of difference. The statement that 'Black feminism is not white feminism' is contingent upon an understanding that Black is not white. However, this representation of the understanding belies a set of complex relations that exceed and transgress any idea that the word 'Black' is bordered off from the word 'white'. Currie explains that 'This suggests that the meaning of words inheres in their relations with each other, that words have no foundations, and meanings are not self-contained' (Currie, 2004: 2).

The slippage of 'not'

The words 'Black' and 'white' are understood in relation to each other. In order to cope with this dialectic of interdependency and the ambivalence, the relation 'must continually produce its slippage, its excess, its difference' (Bhabha, 1994: 86) in order to maintain the construction of difference on axes of inequality. Put simply, the slippage is an inevitable result of maintaining the process of disavowal of the interdependency. In other words, the lack of stability and refusal of 'Black' and 'white' to be contained produces a slip. In the authority and directness of her rhetoric, Lorde does not appear to be slip-sliding, and she shows no hint of uncertainty or of being undecided in her statement that 'Black feminism is not white feminism in blackface'.

A close re-reading of the statement reveals the quandary of giving voice to the specificity of particular entrapments, while also giving voice to the interdependency of difference. Probyn (1993: 120) puts it neatly: 'Without her I'm nothing.' Butler explains how the process of becoming 'nothing' happens, and she argues that the interdependency of difference is an 'undoing': 'I tell a story about the relations I choose, only to expose, somewhere along the way, the way I am gripped and undone by these very relations ... Let's face it. We're undone by each other' (Butler, 2004: 23). However, 'stricken by an indeterminacy' (Bhabha, 1994: 86), or stricken 'with signs of its undoing' (Butler, 2004: 23), the 'not' in 'Black feminism is not white feminism in blackface' is undone and fails. This failure is the slippage and excess referred to by Bhabha earlier, and this produces anxiety. It must be noted that, although Bhabha is referring to the situation of colonization, and to the power relations between the colonizer and the colonized, application to the context of Black feminism and white feminism must include both Black and white feminisms as implicated. The idea of interdependency implies mutuality, and Black and white feminisms/feminists are undone by each other.

'Black feminism is not white feminism in blackface' focusses the gaze on recognition and cautions against misrecognition. It appears that Lorde invites a scrutiny of the real 'blackface'. Lorde seems to be implying the existence and, therefore, the possibility of recognition of the genuine from the imitation. This raises the problem of the construction, constitution and claim of authenticity. Spivak comments that 'what I find useful is the sustained and developing work on the *mechanics* of the constitution of the Other; we can use it to much greater analytic and interventionist advantage than invocations of the *authenticity* of the Other' (Spivak, 1988: 294; emphasis in original). Rather than debating whether or not Lorde is claiming a position of authenticity, Spivak directs the line of interrogation into the mechanics of the authentic. This would lead to questions about the production, function and contingencies of the construction of authenticity.

The anxious desire for recognition of that self-conscious difference, which is not an impersonation or parody of a stereotype, is an aspect of the 'psychic life of power' and an entrapment. Butler comments that 'what is exteriorized or performed can only be understood by reference to what is barred from performance, what cannot or will not be performed' (Butler, 1997a: 144). Impersonations of 'blackface' function in relation to the 'blackface' that has been barred. Indeed, the situation of 'barred' implies that there is something to be barred. The word 'barred' is, therefore, inextricably bound to other contexts, meanings and words – some of which may be present and/or absent, available and/or unavailable, and close and/or distant. This complexity troubles the notion of recognition because, having questioned the notion of a distinction between the real and false 'blackface', the predicament is also one of recognition constituted on misrecognition, just as presence and absence are mutually constitutive. So, the dialectic of 'Black feminism is not white feminism in blackface' is: who or what is constituting, and recognizing, who or what? Lorde comments that 'We have recognized and negotiated these differences, even when this recognition only continued the old dominant/subordinate mode of human relationship, where the oppressed must recognize the masters' difference in order to survive' (Lorde, 1980a: 122). Perhaps engagement with, rather than disavowal of, the dialectics of recognition would form a stronger basis for disrupting 'the old dominant/subordinate' positions.

Fanon and Lorde

Butler's *The Psychic Life of Power* (1997a) enables a shift in gaze from black and white skin colour to a gaze on the mechanisms through which power interpellates the psyche. Thus, the question is not whether a psyche is, or becomes, Black or white, but how the signifiers 'Black' and 'white' are used by the 'psychic life of power'. Moreover, Seshadri-Crooks' analysis of *Recitatif* (Morrison, 1983) and the film *Suture* (1993) 'problematizes the referent, or the body as a site of knowledge' (Seshadri-Crooks, 2000a: 148). Butler's question of 'What is the psychic form that power takes?' (Butler, 1997a: 2) is helpful in the project of understanding further the nuances and implications of 'Black feminism is not white feminism in blackface'. Butler's focus on the relationship between the psyche and power (Butler, 1997a: 3), and on how subjectivity is constituted through the 'psychic life of power', moves the enquiry beyond the regime of visibility. Similarly, Oliver calls for 'a theory that operates between the psyche and the social, through which the very terms of psychoanalysis are transformed into social concepts' (Oliver, 2004: xiv).

Having established that recruitment and 'passionate attachment' (Butler, 1997a: 7) mean that the getting 'in' is different for Black and white people even though they are constituted by, and through, each other, the question is: how does the social get into the psyche in order to create and transform? Fanon's *Black Skin, White Masks* (2008) is a detailed study of the colonization of psychic space as an entrapment of the 'psychic life of power'. Fanon states in his introduction: 'I believe that only a psychoanalytical interpretation of the black problem can lay bare the anomalies of affect that are responsible for the structure of the complex' (Fanon, 2008: 3).

I now move on in this chapter to juxtapose *Black Skin, White Masks*, 'a clinical study' to analyse the 'psychoexistential complex' (Fanon, 2008: 5), with Lorde's Black lesbian feminist, political essays in *Sister Outsider* (1984). The aim of this juxtaposition is to explore the manoeuvres of the 'psychic life of power' and, specifically, to trace the particular entrapments used in the colonization of psychic space. This juxtaposition enables this line of inquiry to move from the regime of visibility, and the issue of recognition and misrecognition, to an analysis of how and why 'Black feminism is not white feminism in blackface' because of what gets under, and goes on under, the skin. Butler (1997a: 19) speaks about the 'process of incorporation' to better understand and formulate questions about how power uses the psychic topography. Butler states that:

> If forms of regulatory power are sustained in part through the formation of a subject, and if that formation takes place according to the requirements of power, specifically, as the incorporation of norms, then a theory of subject formation must give an account of this process of incorporation, and the notion of incorporation must be interrogated to ascertain the psychic topography it assumes.
>
> (Butler, 1997a: 19)

Where Butler speaks of 'incorporation', Fanon (2008: 4) speaks of 'epidermalization' in relation to the specificity of racism. Fanon's concept of 'epidermalization' is particularly useful because it includes an equation of the regime of visibility, the psyche and the social. In this equation, the black epidermis cannot be mimicked because the process of incorporation that regulates the psychic topography forms particular subjectivities.

In *Black Skins, White Masks*, Fanon uses the term 'epidermalization' to describe the process whereby:

> If there is an inferiority complex, it is the outcome of a double process:
> —primarily, economic;
> —subsequently, the internalization – or, better, the epidermalization – of this inferiority
>
> (Fanon, 2008: 4)

More specifically, Fanon talks about 'a racial epidermal schema' (Fanon, 2008: 84). Oliver explains this as the process whereby, in racism, 'the body becomes nothing more than skin, abjected by dominant culture, alien to the one whose bodily integrity it paradoxically both protects and destroys' (Oliver, 2001: 25).

Lorde invokes this racial bodily schema, recalling her own experience:

> Did *bad* mean *Black*? The endless scrubbing with lemon juice in the cracks and crevices of my ripening, darkening, body. And oh, the sins of my dark elbows and knees, my gums and nipples, the folds of my neck and the cave of my armpits!
>
> (Lorde, 1983a: 149, emphasis in original)

Deconstructing this quote, the black epidermis becomes the site where experience, affect, sexuality, the psychic relation to sin and the concept of '*bad*' are represented. Examining the syntax of Lorde's description here and the relations between the words, it could be argued that the spaces in the 'cracks', 'crevices', 'folds' and 'cave' personify what Bhabha describes as 'an interstitial space for the negotiation of meaning, value, judgement – how the "one" survives in/of the "other" as a kind of structure of doubling (not sublimation or sublation) – not pluralism, but excessive iteration' (Seshadri-Crooks, 2000b: 376). Lorde's description summons identification, desire and the gap or slippage of the 'not' in 'Black feminism is not white feminism in blackface'. Bhabha explains:

> For the image – as point of identification – marks the site of an ambivalence. Its representation is always spatially split – it makes *present* something that is *absent* [...] The image is at once a metaphoric substitution, an illusion of presence and by that same token a metonym, a sign of its absence and loss.
>
> (Bhabha, 1986: xxx; emphasis in original)

The relevance of Fanon's work lies in his examination of the process of incorporation as an aspect of the psychic life of racism. Similar to Lorde, Fanon identifies and investigates how the 'entrapments used to neutralize' (Lorde, 1980a: 118) Black people within racism are different than those for white people.

Neither Lorde nor Fanon is saying that racism only affects Black people; their emphasis is on how the entrapments of the 'psychic life of power' operate differently depending on how skin colour is positioned and represented. Both Lorde and Fanon analyze how 'racist social structures create racist psychic structures' (Oliver, 2001: 34). The key point is that the way in which 'racist social structures create racist psychic structures' operates differently for Black and white people.

Furthermore, the intersection of the psychic and the social troubles the borders that are often created between the two: for example, as reflected in disciplinary borders that demarcate the social to the sociological and the psyche to the psychological. Butler argues that the 'process of internalization *fabricates the distinction between interior and exterior life*' (Butler, 1997a: 19; emphasis in original). Butler elaborates her analysis to add further layers of complexity:

> Where social categories guarantee a recognizable and enduring social existence, the embrace of such categories, even if they work in the service of subjection, is often preferred to no social existence at all. How is it, then, that the longing for subjection, based on a longing for social existence, recalling and exploiting primary dependencies, emerges as an instrument and effect of the power of subjection?
>
> (Butler, 1997a: 20)

A close re-reading of Lorde's and Fanon's experiences of racism provides a powerful response to Butler's difficult questions. Fanon explains:

> ... I begin to suffer from not being a white man to the degree that the white man imposes discrimination on me, makes me a colonized native, robs me of all worth, all individuality, tells me that I am a parasite on the world, that I must bring myself as quickly as possible into step with the white world, "that I am a brute beast, that my people and I are like a walking dung-heap that disgustingly fertilizes sweet sugar cane and silky cotton, that I have no use in the world." Then I will quite simply try to make myself white: that is, I will compel the white man to acknowledge that I am human.
>
> (Fanon, 2008: 73)

A re-reading of Fanon through a re-reading of Lorde opens up interesting dimensions of analysis in relation to Butler's comment that 'the desire to survive, "to be," is a pervasively exploitable desire. The one who holds out the promise of continued existence plays to the desire to survive' (Butler, 1997a: 7).

Drawing on her experience as a child, Lorde's description in the following passage brings together desire, epidermalization/racial bodily schema and dehumanization:

> ... the stormy little Black girl who once longed to be white or anything other than who she was, since all she was ever allowed to be was the

sum of the color of her skin and the textures of her hair, the shade of her knees and elbows, and those things were clearly not acceptable as human.

(Lorde, 1983a: 174)

Butler explains:

> ... if following Foucault, we understand power as *forming* the subject as well, as providing the very condition of its existence and the trajectory of its desire, then power is not simply what we oppose but also, in a strong sense, what we depend on for our existence ... the "we" who accept such terms are fundamentally dependent on those terms for "our" existence.
>
> (Butler, 1997a: 2; emphasis in original)

Fanon is clear that the imposed 'terms' of being 'a parasite', of 'no use', robbed of 'all worth, all individuality', 'a brute beast' and 'a walking dung-heap' (Fanon, 2008: 73) provide compelling motivation and rationale for coming into step with the very world that imposed the 'terms' to 'make myself white' (Fanon, 2008: 73). The terms of what is 'allowed' and 'acceptable' (Lorde, 1983a: 174) as products of racist ideology 'enter the colonized through the skin' (Oliver, 2004: 51). Both Fanon and Lorde establish the inextricable interdependency between ideology, embodiment and the 'psychic life of power'.

Resisting the terms of oppression

If feminism (or, indeed, any liberation ideology) is a political movement that questions and resists terms of oppression, and if these terms are different for Black and white women, it follows that Black feminism requires a questioning of, and resistance to, different terms than white feminism. A close re-reading of Lorde's 'not in blackface' is exactly this questioning and resistance to the terms invoked in the racist regimes of visibility, and in the process of epidermalization, whereby 'stereotypes of inferiority are absorbed into the skin' (Oliver, 2001: 24). Thus, Lorde uses the trope, but extends the analysis beyond mimicry to indicate a refusal to 'make myself white' (Fanon, 2008: 73) in 'blackface'. Butler comments that:

> If, as Norma Alarcón has insisted, women of color are "multiply inter-pellated," called by many names, constituted in and by that multiple calling, then this implies that the symbolic domain, the domain of socially instituted norms, is composed of *racializing norms*, and that they exist not merely alongside gender norms, but are articulated

through one another. Hence it is no longer possible to make sexual difference prior to racial difference or, for that matter, to make them into fully separable axes of social regulation and power.

(Butler, 1993b: 279; emphasis in original)

'Black feminism is not white feminism in blackface' both acknowledges the psychic life of racism and resists its terms simultaneously. In using the term 'blackface', Lorde is perhaps saying 'beware of mimicry, beware of masquerades and of how the almost' (Bhabha, 1994: 86) has to continually produce its slippage. The reasons to be so suspicious of such mimicry are because:

- mimicry is one of the entrapments used to neutralize Black and white women. Here, the following words of Lorde are relevant: '*the master's tools will never dismantle the master's house*' (Lorde, 1979a: 112; emphasis in original);
- mimicry defends against the painful wrench of undoing the recruitment and 'passionate attachment'. Mimicry allows the masquerade of an unaltered, altered position;
- mimicry makes collusion with oppression more palatable;
- the 'almost the same' (Bhabha, 1994: 86) both establishes and shrinks the gap between different subjects, making unbearable relationality more bearable. Well, the 'almost the same' means that there is less need to interrogate the construction of difference.

Very dangerous territory, indeed!

Conclusion

'Black feminism is not white feminism in blackface' could translate to say 'Black-women-only feminist spaces and services are not white women feminist spaces and services in blackface'. Changing the face does not fundamentally change the object beneath. It does not alter the hailing and does nothing to alter the unequal power differentials that racism requires. It is like 'the phantom of the opera' – still ugly beneath the mask. This is why 'Black feminism is not white feminism in blackface' has nothing and everything to do with the colour of skin. Thus, this is why Black-women-only spaces and services have nothing and everything to do with the colour of skin. Or, in the words of Lorde:

I urge each one of us here to reach down into that deep place of knowl-edge inside herself and touch that terror and loathing of any difference that lives there. See whose face it wears. Then the personal as the political can begin to illuminate all our choices.

(Lorde, 1979a: 113; emphasis in original)

The future of our earth may depend upon the ability of all women to identify and develop new definitions of power and new patterns of relating across difference ... The old patterns, no matter how cleverly rearranged to imitate progress, still condemn us to cosmetically altered repetitions of the same old exchanges, the same old guilt, hatred, recrimination, lamentation and suspicion.

(Lorde, 1980a: 123)

Notes

1 The location of the hyphen in the term 'Black-women-only' (rather than 'Black women-only') is particularly important and a deliberate intervention to communicate clearly that the intersectional experience of being both Black and a woman is greater than the sum of race and gender (Crenshaw, 1989).
2 Debates about the need for women-only spaces have been present in critical psychology. Parker notes: 'One of the particular struggles feminist psychologists have had to engage in has been around the right to organize separately as women. In some contexts, such as the UK, it has been necessary to argue that there is a specific intellectual domain that needs a distinct academic organization. In other contexts, such as Scandinavia, women's organization in psychology has been under cover of union activity, and it is then also possible to connect with wider questions of oppression and practice beyond the discipline' (Parker, 1999: 6).
3 Equality Act 2010; Race Equality Duty within the Race Relations (Amendment) Act 2000; and the Gender Equality Duty within the Equality Act 2006, amending the (Sex Discrimination Act).

Women-only services: making the case. A guide for women's organisations (Women's Resource Centre, 2011);
The Impact of the Equality Act 2010 on Charities (Morris et al., 2013).
4 Kaur and Shah (on the application of) vs. London borough of Ealing [2008] EWHC 2062 (Admin).

4   The aporetics of intersectionality

This chapter addresses key issues that Hook raises in his statement that:

> ... we need strong psychological accounts of racism if racism is to be adequately examined, confronted and hence contested ... Indeed, by neglecting the psychological/psychical as a critical means of explanation and/or critique, critical psychology seems to have undermined its own critical efficacy regards the phenomena of racism. Oddly, the focus on the turn to text that has proved so central to its efforts in the last decade might represent its most pronounced critical limitation, especially so if these efforts have become largely limited to the discursive as its conceptual and methodological analytical mode of choice, to conceiving of racism as an issue of representation, rhetorical strategy, significatory practice, etc.
>
> (Hook, 2005: n.p.)

In terms of methodology, this chapter remains with 'the turn to text' in a close re-reading of Lorde in order to critically analyse 'the affective and psychological components of the political phenomenon of racism' (Hook, 2005: n.p.). Furthermore, written in the first person, as a deeply personal, reflective engagement with 'the personalized affectivity of racism, the individualized psychical mechanics that underscore its discursive functioning' (Hook, 2005: n.p.), this chapter occupies '[t]he tensions of writing from a subject position within impersonal writing [which] constitutes a contradiction, but it is one that I think mirrors theorizing from contradictory locations' (Collins, 1998: xxi). As will become evident, the issues of occupancy, location and position are core to my reflective analysis of personalized affectivity of the racist, homophobic patriarchy I inhabit.

'*I* have to work on integration for myself. *You* have to do it for yourself'

> CR: Here's a question that I want to ask you, partly because it's been a big problem to me and I'd like to know how you have handled it. Being black, a lesbian, and a feminist puts you in a position where you have to deal with what, at times, appear to be three mutually exclusive ideologies or priorities. How do you manage to integrate them all ... or do you?
>
> AL: Well, Cheryl, as I'm sure you know, it has felt, at different points in my life, like every single way in which I would identify myself was in total conflict with every other way. First of all, there's always going to be some group or some person who wants you to talk from only one particular perspective. That's very destructive. It's like putting all the eggs in one basket. It also reduces you to one component, and it's just such a terrible injustice to all the other pieces of yourself. It cuts me off from the energy that comes from all those different pieces. So integration is absolutely necessary. *I* have to work on integration for myself. *You* have to do it for yourself. What I've learned, and this was indeed a learning process, is that it is absolutely essential not to allow pieces of myself to be at war with each other ... But as long as you let yourself be baffled, as long as you let one piece of yourself be cancelled out by another, you will always be subject to the kind of turmoil that sucks energy away. It's hard, it's very hard. But it's not harder than the way they want us to live, which is in categories. And, it's far more productive.

> (Savren & Robinson, 1982: 81–2; ellipses and emphasis in original)

Although Lorde did not use the term 'intersectionality', it is clear from her life and works that she refused to 'pluck out some one aspect of myself and present this as the meaningful whole, eclipsing or denying the other parts of self' (Lorde, 1980a: 120).

The elements, essence and conceptual framework of the term 'intersectionality' have evolved through, and are evident in, Black feminist writing and testimony. It is within this historical, social and political context that Crenshaw coined the term 'intersectionality' in her 1989 seminal work entitled, 'Demarginalizing the Intersection of Race and Sex: A Black Feminist Critique of Antidiscrimination Doctrine, Feminist Theory and Antiracist Politics'. In this paper, Crenshaw uses intersectionality as a critical lens within the context of the US legal framework with regard to discrimination and, as such, intersectionality offers a powerful tool for feminist legal theory, critical race theory and critical legal studies. There is a growing body of scholarship in some branches of psychology and mental health that point to the importance of intersectionality as an invaluable tool for critical analysis of simultaneous, multiple structural discrimination (E.R. Cole, 2009; Mens-Verhulst & Radtke, 2006, 2008). Indeed, recent evaluations of the conceptual framework of intersectionality indicate the reach, importance and relevance of intersectionality in current debates (Burman, 2004; Davis, 2008; Grzanka, 2014; Lutz *et al*., 2011; McCall, 2005; Nash, 2008; Pateman & Mills, 2007; Phoenix & Pattynama, 2006; Taylor *et al*., 2010) and scholarship, including the introduction in 2012 of *Intersectionalities: A Global Journal of Social Work Analysis, Research, Polity and Practice*.

Territorial disputes over who owns the term 'intersectionality' and where the term originated not only function as a distraction from the point of Crenshaw's paper, but also function to establish and maintain the very notion of separate borders that Crenshaw contested. The splits between analyses of the structural and analyses of the subject/subjective/subjectivity, using intersectionality, run counter to the spirit of intersectionality.

This chapter picks up on three specific components of Lorde's reply to Robinson's question quoted earlier. The objectives of this chapter (in no specific order because the components under examination are mutually constitutive) are: first, I want to understand the nature of the turmoil, or why 'It's hard, it's very hard' (Savren & Robinson, 1982: 81) to 'integrate all the parts of who I am, openly, allowing power from particular sources of my living to flow back and forth freely through all my different selves, without the restrictions of externally imposed definition' (Lorde, 1980a: 120); second, I want to understand the nature and function of the 'terrible injustice' of living in categories (Savren & Robinson, 1982: 81); third, I want to understand what is productive about integration.

Intersectionality: an experience of aporia

This reflective analysis examines the challenge I confront as a Black lesbian feminist in trying to 'integrate all the parts of who I am' (Lorde, 1980a: 120). This chapter picks up on Lorde's reply to Robinson that '*I* have to work on integration for myself. *You* have to do it for yourself' (Savren & Robinson, 1982: 81; emphasis in original) in an effort to understand better the personal, political task of doing intersectionality *for* myself and *within* myself. The challenge turns out to be more complicated and more emotionally difficult when integrating becomes the task of intersecting all the parts of 'who I am', and when those parts of who I am are constituted as the stranger within (Kristeva, 1991).

This chapter concentrates on two intersecting aspects of the challenge: first, I argue that any attempt to dismantle borders constructed to separate out categories of experience and identity bumps up against a number of interconnected aporia; second, I argue that the emotional task and experience of intersecting 'all my different selves' (Lorde, 1980a: 121) across psychic borders have a 'psychological toll' (The Combahee River Collective, 1977: 266). Lorde describes the difficulty in the following way:

> It was hard enough to be Black, to be Black and female, to be Black, female, and gay. To be Black, female, gay, and out of the closet in a white environment, even to the extent of dancing in the Bagatelle, was considered by many Black lesbians to be simply suicidal.
>
> (Lorde, 1996: 195)

The point is that it is the experience of aporia that produces the psychological turmoil. Any attempt at a 'psychic retreat' (Steiner, 1993: 1) from the 'psychological toll' of aporia is merely to disavow the aporia. Royle defines aporia as 'loosely a rhetorical term for "doubt" or "difficulty in choosing", but more precisely it means a sort of absolute blockage, a "No Way"' (Royle, 2003: 92).

This chapter seeks to use aporia as the site and method for the '*You* have to do it for yourself' (Savren & Robinson, 1982: 81; emphasis in original) experience of intersectionality. Speaking of all experience, Derrida asks: 'Can one speak – and if so, in what sense – of an *experience of the aporia*? An experience *of the aporia as such*? Or vice versa: Is an experience possible that would not be an experience of the aporia?' (Derrida, 1993: 15; emphasis in original). As will become evident through this chapter, it is the experience of the 'impossible' in the aporia that creates the conditions for the 'possible' and the 'productive'. The graft of the 'psychological toll' (The Combahee River Collective, 1977: 266) in negotiating the aporia opens up opportunities for an indeterminate becoming. Emphasis must be placed here on the word 'indeterminate' because intersectionality and the aporia are both constituted by, and contingent upon, the indeterminate. I argue that it is engagement with the indeterminate that produces the transformation that is core to the activism of Black feminist theory. Furthermore, transforming the 'terrible injustice' (Savren & Robinson, 1982: 81) of that which has been determined for Black women into a shifting indeterminate is the basis for an ethical, productive encounter.

The challenge of Crenshaw's theory of intersectionality is the challenge presented in the aphorism, 'the personal is the political'. Intersectionality goes beyond merely combining inadequate and oppressive socio-economic, political and legal structures, and inadequate feminist theories and practices.

With regard to this point, Collins offers a useful distinction between intersectionality and her own concept of the matrix of domination:

> ... I use and distinguish between both terms in examining how oppression affects Black women. Intersectionality refers to particular forms of intersecting oppressions, for example, intersections of race and gender, or of sexuality and nation. Intersectional paradigms remind us that oppression cannot be reduced to one fundamental type, and that oppressions work together in producing injustice. In contrast, the matrix of domination refers to how these intersecting oppressions are actually organized.
>
> (Collins, 2000: 18)

I want to think of intersectionality in the light of Butler's comment that 'Such a project requires thinking the theory of power together with a theory of the psyche ... power that at first appears as external, pressed upon the subject, pressing the subject into subordination, assumes a psychic form that constitutes the subject's self-identity' (Butler, 1997a: 3). This chapter proposes and interrogates the 'psychic form' of intersectionality that 'constitutes the subject's self-identity' in two ways that are interconnected: first, the analysis dismantles the conceptual structure of intersectionality to show that it is bound up with the aporia of hospitality and borders in an effort to contain the anxiety generated by the foreign stranger within me; second, the analysis examines how and why the intersection of selves that constitutes a self is so emotionally difficult. I want to understand how and why my emotional experience of the impact of intersectionality feels like Kristeva's description:

> Confronting the foreigner whom I reject and with whom at the same time I identify, I lose my boundaries, I no longer have a container, the memory of experiences when I had been abandoned overwhelm me, I lose my composure. I feel "lost," "indistinct," "hazy."
>
> (Kristeva, 1991: 187)

The aporia of intersectionality as method and content

This chapter brings together conceptual frameworks from Crenshaw, Derrida and Lorde as theoretical lenses across temporal and spatial theoretical borders. Although they may appear to speak in different tongues, have different traditions and standpoints, and could be seen as foreigners to each other, I suggest that Crenshaw, Derrida and Lorde have a shared concern with intersectionality, and each provide ways to approach the challenges of intersectionality. In terms of methodology, this chapter is an intersection of approaches to intersectionality. It is a deliberate transgression of borders to attempt a space of emotional and 'intellectual hospitality' (Bennett, 2003 and Kaufman, 2001, cited in Molz & Gibson, 2007: 2) because 'what is at stake is not only the thinking *of* hospitality, but thinking *as* hospitality' (Friese, 2004, cited in Molz & Gibson, 2007: 2; emphasis in original).

It will become evident that both the subject under analysis and the method used to examine the subject under analysis mirror each other. The subject under examination is the challenge of Crenshaw's (1989) theory of intersectionality in relation to 'mutually exclusive categories of experience and analysis' (Crenshaw, 1989: 139). To be more specific, the challenge under examination is neither the identification nor naming of the exclusive categories of identity, nor is it concerned with proving that particular categories exist; the challenge under examination is the exclusivity of the categories, or how and why the categories are bordered off from each other so that the separateness serves to maintain exclusivity. These borders between categories of experience and analysis are maintained even when the cost is erasure of 'conceptualization, identification and remediation of race and sex discrimination by limiting inquiry' (Crenshaw, 1989: 140). The subject under analysis has the construction of borders and the maintenance of exclusive categories as core elements. Derrida's work exposes that the complication is in the construction itself, and this is demonstrated in the inherent aporia of borders, categories and exclusivity. The theory of intersectionality effectively challenges mutually exclusive categories of experience and analysis. The theory of intersectionality successfully exposes that these are socially constructed borders of experience and analysis, and goes on to detail the destructive negative consequences of separated out categories. However, and this is the crux of this chapter, intersectionality does not resolve the aporia.

As a Black lesbian feminist, my emotional struggle to tolerate[1] the intersection of experience, and even desiring the fragmented parts of self to touch each other, come up against the aporia of borders and the aporia of hospitality. However, it is precisely within the indeterminate space of the aporia that the potential for an ethical, accountable relation to self can be experienced. In other words, what is being proposed is the idea of the 'possible' within the 'impossible'. Within the context of this chapter, the 'possible' refers to Black women's resistance to fixed, stable, totalized identity formations imposed by a racist, homophobic patriarchy. I contend that multiple and intersecting aporia create, rather than foreclose, the revolutionary potential of the activism of Black feminist theory. The task of confronting prior decided horizons of 'representational realism' (Wilkinson & Kitzinger, 1996: 15) is the task of enduring the experience and experiment of the undecidable. Derrida states: 'I will even venture to say that ethics, politics, and responsibility, *if there are any*, will only ever have begun with the experience and experiment of the aporia' (Derrida, 1992b: 41; emphasis in original).

Inhabiting intersectionality

Lorde's work is primarily focussed on the tribulations of relating across difference and transgressing externally imposed ideological, structural, emotional and psychic borders used to separate, distort and fragment. Lorde explains the focus of her work in the following, succinct summary:

> My writing is about difference. My writing is about how we learn to lie down with the different parts of ourselves, so that we can in fact learn to respect and honor the different parts of each other so that we in fact can learn how to use them, moving toward something that needs to be done, that has never been done before.
>
> (Abod, 1987: 158)

Of significance to my analysis is the way that Lorde prescribes the intersectional experience as a condition for moving toward the unknown and the unexpected. Derrida states that 'If there were a horizon of expectation, if there were anticipation or programming, there would be neither event nor history' (Derrida & Stiegler, 2002: 12).

My primary concern is to better understand why it is so difficult to 'learn to lie down with the different parts of ourselves' (Abod, 1987: 158) in order to transgress internal, apparently mutually exclusive, categories of experience and analysis. My concern is to find assistance in the sustained fight against seductive, comfortable resolutions to an already difficult life in a racist, homophobic patriarchy. Lorde outlines the dangers in the following caution:

> And make no mistake; you will be paid well not to feel, not to scrutinize the function of your differences and their meaning, until it will be too late to feel at all. You will be paid in insularity, in poisonous creature comforts, false securities, in the spurious belief that the midnight knock will always be upon somebody else's door.
>
> (Lorde, n.d.: 204)

I want to better understand the emotional difficulty of embodied intersectionality. I find Alcoff's development of Merleau-Ponty's idea of the 'habitual body' in her article 'Towards a Phenomenology of Racial Embodiment' (Alcoff, 1999) useful in thinking of intersecting vectors of identity categories inhabiting the body and constituted of bodily experience. The concept of the 'habitual body' picks up on the intersection of inhabitance and habit, where the ideas of location and conditioning are inextricably linked.

The relevance of focussing on the embodied, emotional experience of the aporia of intersectionality is revealed in the meaning of the word itself. The etymology of aporia is from the Greek 'aporos', which, when spilt into its two morphemes, *a* and *porous*, means 'without' and 'passage' so that 'aporos' comes to mean 'impassable' (Royle, 2003: 92). From *poros* we get the word *pore* or *pores*, conjuring the idea of 'passage' from the inside to the outside of the body and vice-versa. Thus, in the context of the body, *poros* comes to mean a passage that stimulates circulation and flow, and a type of bodily breathing that denotes a healthy living organism. However, I want to use Crenshaw's theory of intersectionality alongside Derrida's theory of aporia to contend that it is in the 'without passage', or it is in the 'impassable' indeterminacy of intersectionality: that our 'fullest concentration of energy is available' (Lorde, 1980a: 120). However, the point is not to rank the indeterminacy of *aporos* above the determinacy of *poros*, or vice-versa, but to see these terms as mutually contingent. Resorting to the configuration of a binary opposition of determinacy and indeterminacy is to miss the productive space of the dialectic.

Mairs explains that 'The body itself is a dwelling place, as the Anglo-Saxons knew in naming it *banhus* (bonehouse) and *lichama* (bodyhome)' (Mairs, 1989: 471; italics in original). For as long as I inhabit my body, the subject of this chapter inhabits me. It has become, and continues to be, my home; or, in Lorde's words, 'in my journey to this house of myself' (Lorde, 1996: 31). So, I say to you and to myself, 'Welcome, make yourself at home; my home is your home' and, yet, as will become evident, this is impossible. The impossibility of this invitation of hospitality is concerned with the relationship between host and guest inextricably bound up with the aporia of borders.

My argument is that the impossibility of hospitality functions within the 'bodyhome' between the different, intersecting elements of my subjectivity as a Black lesbian feminist. The attempts of my race, gender, class, sexuality and age to play host and guest to each other across multiple borders, within the territory of my psyche, are caught up in Derrida's problematic, 'Is not hospitality an interruption of the self?' (Derrida, 1999: 51).

The psychological toll of intersectionality

This is not a comfortable scrutiny. Even though it takes work to understand and communicate what is wrong with a single axis framework, it is, perhaps, harder to feel directly and fully that the 'intersectional experience is greater than the sum of racism and sexism' (Crenshaw, 1989: 140). The intersectional experience can be emotionally overwhelming. I am reminded of Lorde's questions: 'How much of this truth can I bear to see/ and still live/ unblinded?/ How much of this pain/ can I use?' (Lorde, 1979d: 106).

The following excerpts from Crenshaw's (1989) paper highlight the function of borders within constructions of identity categories that the concept of intersectionality seeks to contest. The 'tightly-drawn parameters' (152), 'normative vision' (145), 'filtered through categorical analyses that completely obscure' (149–50), notions of discrimination 'narrowly tailored to embrace only a small set of circumstances' (151), 'separate spheres ideology' (154) and 'limited view' (145) that 'erases Black women in the conceptualization, identification and remediation of race and sex discrimination' (140) serve me very well in mitigating threatening collisions of exhaustion, vulnerability, pain, hatred and anger located firmly within my patrolled psychic borders. There are times when I 'hide behind the mockeries of separations that have been imposed upon us' (Lorde, 1977: 43) and ignore the 'fallacies of separatist solutions' (Lorde, 1979b: 61). The tension of the task is articulated by Lorde, on the one hand: 'My fullest concentration of energy is available to me only when I integrate all the parts of who I am, openly, allowing power from particular sources of my living to flow back and forth freely through all my different selves' (Lorde, 1980a: 120–1); while, on the other hand: 'And of course I am afraid, because the transformation of silence into language and action is an act of self-revelation, and that always seems fraught with danger' (Lorde, 1977: 42).

The challenge of the activism of Black feminist theory is in relation to external racist, homophobic, patriarchal structures of oppression, but is also equally in relation to my own internal, psychological self and our internal, psychological selves as Black women. Lorde points out that 'It is easier to deal with the external manifestations of racism and sexism than it is to deal with the results of those distortions internalized within our consciousness of ourselves and one another' (Lorde, 1983a: 147).

Learning from the Combahee River Collective

The Combahee River Collective[2] has given us one of the most articulate and comprehensive statements of the necessity for, and difficulty of being in, Black feminist activist spaces. The position and explanation of intersectionality in the very first paragraph of *A Black Feminist Statement* (The Combahee River Collective, 1977) emphasizes the importance of the intersectional experience to the Collective's existence and mission:

> ... we are actively committed to struggling against racial, sexual, heterosexual, and class oppression and see as our particular task the development of integrated analysis and practice based upon the fact that the major systems of oppression are interlocking. The synthesis of

these oppressions creates the conditions of our lives. As Black women we see Black feminism as the logical political movement to combat the manifold and simultaneous oppressions that all women of color face.

(The Combahee River Collective, 1977: 261)

However, any notion, myth or fantasy that Black feminist spaces and experiences are comfortable, cosy, safe and secure is false. The Combahee River Collective makes this point clear: 'The overwhelming feeling that we had is that after years and years we had finally found each other' (1977: 268). However, at the same time, the Combahee River Collective also acknowledges that 'The psychological toll of being a Black woman and the difficulties this presents in reaching political consciousness and doing political work can never be underestimated' (1977: 266). The Combahee River Collective (1977) identifies a number of reasons for the difficulty:

There is a very low value placed upon Black women's psyches in this society, which is both racist and sexist.

(p. 266)

... it calls into question some of the most basic assumptions about our existence ...

(p. 267)

The material conditions of most Black women would hardly lead them to upset both economic and sexual arrangements that seem to represent some stability in their lives.

(p. 267)

Many Black women have a good understanding of both sexism and racism, but because of the everyday constrictions of their lives cannot risk struggling against them both.

(p. 267)

In addition to this list, Lorde adds:

... we have *all* been programmed to respond to the human differences between us with fear and loathing ... we have no patterns for relating across our human differences as equals.

(Lorde, 1980a: 115; emphasis in original)

... the true focus of revolutionary change is never merely the oppressive situations which we seek to escape, but that piece of the oppressor which is planted deep within each of us, and which knows only the oppressors' tactics, the oppressors' relationships.

(Lorde, 1980a: 123)

Both Lorde and the Combahee River Collective make reference to Black women's experience of feeling 'crazy' within the distorted perspectives of a racist, homophobic patriarchy. For example, Lorde states:

... I wanted to say to the Black women of London, young Black women with whom I was in contact; it is not all in your head. Don't let them muck around with your realities. You may not be able to make very much inroad, but at least you've got to stop feeling quite so crazy. Because, after a while, constantly exposed to unacknowledged racism, Black women get to feeling really crazy. And then, it's all in our heads, the white women say.

(Parmar & Kay, 1988: 175)

The Combahee River Collective states:

Black feminists often talk about their feelings of craziness before becoming conscious of the concepts of sexual politics, patriarchal rule, and, most importantly, feminism, the political analysis and practice that we women use to struggle against our oppression.

(1977: 263)

After arguing that 'Black feminism is not white feminism in blackface' (Lorde, 1979b: 60), after arguing that 'the entrapments used to neutralize Black and white women are not the same' (Lorde, 1980a: 118), after arguing that 'beyond sisterhood is still racism' (Lorde, 1979c: 70) and after arguing for structures, ideology and spaces to attend to the intersection of simultaneous, multiple oppression, finally we actually obtain Black feminist spaces and services – a space longed for, rare and often unfamiliar; we are left with ourselves and each other in the space. Lorde reflects: 'I thought, wait a minute, racism doesn't just distort white people – what about us? What about the effects of white racism upon the ways Black people view each other? Racism internalized?' (Lorde, 1979d: 96). Black women are left with the 'psychological toll' (The Combahee River Collective, 1977: 266) of difference, no patterns for relating across difference (Lorde, 1980a: 115) and, furthermore, we are left with the aporia of borders and hospitality.

These tensions do not just inhabit Black feminist spaces, services and scholarship; these tensions are inhabited and inhabit each other. Of course, this is no coincidence given that Black feminist spaces, services and scholarship are born out of subjugated knowledge in the matrix of oppression

(Collins, 2000). In other words, the activism of Black feminist theory arises out of, is understood in terms of, and transforms the daily lived experience of Black women. Lorde states that 'survival isn't theoretical, we live it everyday. We live it on the streets, we live it in the banks, we live it with our children' (Greene, 1989: 183). Thus, and this is a key point, intersectionality is not just theoretical, but rather, the process of surviving the intersectional experience needs to be understood in the context of Black women's lives. Lorde explains: 'those of us who have been forged in the crucibles of difference – those of us who are poor, who are lesbians, who are Black, who are older – know that *survival is not an academic skill*' (Lorde, 1979a: 112; emphasis in original).

Intersecting encounters between Black women

No matter how many times I read *Ain't I a Woman* by hooks (1982), I am overwhelmed by feelings of rage, pain and despair. The emotional impact is traumatic, exhausting and more than I can bear. I am clear that this is not about first-encounter emotional impact, and I know there is no option of desensitization due to familiarity, just as the emotional impact of working in Rape Crisis centres[3] is the same today as it was when I first started 30 years ago. The emotional impact is an intersectional experience. Looking back on writing *Ain't I a Woman*, bell hooks (1989: 151–3) reflects:

> The book emerged out of my longing for self-recovery, for education for critical consciousness – for a way of understanding black female experience that would liberate us from the colonizing mentality fostered in a racist, sexist context.
>
> (p. 151)

> While writing, I often felt an intense despair that was so overwhelming I really questioned how we could bear being alive in this society, how could we stay alive. I was profoundly discouraged by the many forces colluding to support the myth of the strong super-black woman, and it seemed that it would be impossible to compel recognition of black women's exploitation and oppression. It is not that black women have not been and are not strong; it is simply that this is only a part of our story, a dimension, just as the suffering is another dimension – one that has been most unnoticed and unattended to.
>
> (pp. 152–3)

The intersectional experience of living, writing and re-reading *Ain't I a Woman* includes the suffering, exploitation and silencing of Black slave women in conjunction with the physical and emotional toil experienced by the Black feminist, bell hooks. This toil is inextricably entwined with my own encounter as a Black woman, and is a toil that is inextricably entwined with being a Black woman in relation to other Black women in the context of a racist, homophobic patriarchy.

What can be seen at play here is the refusal of intersectionality to be bounded. It is important to understand that although the intersectional experience is greater than the sum of race plus class plus gender plus other constructs of identity, intersectionality is not a unifying mechanism. The political function and lived experience of intersectionality are captured in Derrida's statement: 'What interests me is the limit of every attempt to totalize, to gather, *versammeln* ... the limit of this unifying, uniting movement, the limit that it had to encounter, because the relationship of the unity to itself implies some difference' (Derrida & Caputo, 1997: 13; emphasis in original). What interests me is the emotional difficulty of encountering and resisting the limit that includes my own emotional resistance to the element of unavailability in intersectionality.

The excess of Black women

Furthermore, in the context of a racist, homophobic patriarchy, Black women are constituted as the abject subject defined by Kristeva as 'what disturbs identity, system, order. What does not respect borders, positions, rules. The in-between, the ambiguous, the composite' (Kristeva, 1982: 4). Black women are excess in every sense of Bill Ashcroft's exploration of the word:

> Too much, too long, too many, too subversive, too voluble, too insistent, too loud, too strident, too much-too-much, too complex, too hybrid, too convoluted, too disrespectful, too antagonistic, too insistent, too insistent, too insistent, too repetitive, too paranoid, too ... excessive.
> (Ashcroft, 1994: 33; ellipsis in original)

Each identity category that constitutes the subjectivity of Black women, and each identity category that constitutes me as a Black lesbian feminist, is excessive in itself. The infinite referral and deferral of intersections of excess produce excess, and are felt as an excess. The emotional impact of intersectionality is an excess that I find 'too much-too-much' to bear.

The relation without relation

The intersectional dynamics at work transgress temporal and spatial borders. I find Derrida's statement that '[w]hat disrupts the totality is the condition for the relation to the other' (Derrida & Caputo, 1997: 13) useful when applied to Lorde's example of attending her first job interview:

> My first interview for a part-time job after school. An optical company on Nassau Street has called my school and asked for one of its students. The man behind the counter reads my application and then looks up at me, surprised by my Black face. His eyes remind me of the woman on the train when I was five. Then something else is added, as he looks me up and down, pausing at my breasts.
>
> (Lorde, 1983a: 149)

The intersection of racism and sexism flows across time and space in a performative, embodied experience of infinite intersections. The body, breast and skin are sites of objectification that incorporate being treated as if she were a five-year-old roach (Lorde, 1983a: 147; Lorde, 2000: 149) intersected with hundreds of other inhabited habits of racism, sexism and homophobia experienced by Lorde across her life span, as indicated by the use of the present tense (Ahmed, 2000: 39–40). Lorde is caught in an indeterminate present-to-past, past-to-present relation. Referring to Lévinas' (1969) notion of 'rapport sans rapport,' Derrida explains that:

> The structure of my relation to the other is of a "relation without relation." It is a relation in which the other remains absolutely transcendent. I cannot reach the other. I cannot know the other from the inside and so on.
>
> (Derrida & Caputo, 1997: 14)

What I am trying to demonstrate is that hooks' writing of *Ain't I a Woman*, contingent upon Truth's question, 'Ain't I a Woman?', is inextricably bound with my own personal engagement with *Ain't I a Woman* and with Lorde's encounters as 'the sister outsider'. These intersecting relations are a 'relation without relation' (Derrida & Caputo, 1997: 14), where the relation to the other is an impossible relation to self. Relation without relation is a borderless relation. The infinite intersections remain 'absolutely transcendent' and, although this condition is overwhelmingly destabilizing, it is the very condition of transformation. To return to the quote by Lorde that I used to open this chapter, it is the condition in which 'My fullest concentration of energy is available to me ... allowing power from particular sources of my living to flow back and forth freely through all my different selves' (Lorde, 1980a: 120–1).

Lorde and Derrida each propose a political ethics that resists the limitations of presenting the self as a 'meaningful whole' (Lorde, 1980a: 120). Derrida explains:

> It is because I am not one with myself that I can speak with the other and address the other. That is not a way of avoiding responsibility.

On the contrary, it is the only way for me to take responsibility and to make decisions.

(Derrida & Caputo, 1997: 14)

Derrida's reference to responsibility alludes to a kind of ethics, where the refusal of categories, or refusal of that which is already decided, is the basis for an ethics of decision-making. In the following quote, Lorde brings in the notion of justice:

> I am not one piece of myself. I cannot be simply a Black person and not be a woman too, nor can I be a woman without being a lesbian.... Of course, there'll always be people, and there have always been people in my life, who will come to me and say, "Well, here, define yourself as such and such," to the exclusion of the other pieces of myself. There is an injustice to self in doing this ...
>
> (Evans, 1979: 72)

Intersectionality: the unavailable solution

I find particularly useful the phrase Minh-ha (2011) uses when she speaks of 'the boundary event', conjuring up connotations of the active, productive dynamics of 'event' as something absolutely not static, emphasizing 'boundary' as a verb, not a noun. The 'boundary event' of the activism of Black feminist theory becomes a question of who or what is host and guest in the intersecting borders of my experience and analysis. I propose that host and guest are at the heart of the matter; then, to go a step further, to propose that it is not hospitality, but the 'impossibility' of hospitality that is the issue. Reflecting on my experience as a Black lesbian feminist, it continues to be a training in understanding the 'possible' in the 'impossible'.

This task calls for a rigorous and vigilant resistance to expected solutions, frameworks of thinking and instructions, especially where credibility is contingent upon prior, anticipated expectations. Derrida articulates the caution well:

> The *arrivant* must be absolutely other, the other I expect not to be expecting, that I'm not waiting for, whose expectation is made of a nonexpectation, an expectation without what in philosophy is called a horizon of expectation, when a certain knowledge still anticipates and amortizes in advance. If I am sure that there is going to be an event, this will not be an event.
>
> (Derrida & Stiegler, 2002: 13; italics in original)

In speaking of the journey of the activism of Black feminist theory, Lorde picks up on the idea of the 'horizon of expectation' and, like Derrida, she resists the 'already': 'What you chart is already where you've been. But where we are going, there is no chart yet ... Our Black women's vision has no horizon' (Parmar & Kay, 1988: 180). Furthermore, Spivak speaks of 'a placing forth of the solution as the unavailability of a unified solution to a unified or homogeneous, generating or receiving, consciousness. This unavailability is often not confronted. It is dodged and the problem apparently solved' (Spivak, 1985: 55). In accordance with Spivak, this chapter attempts to trace the solution of 'unavailability' in intersectionality not in order to discredit intersectionality as a solution, but rather, to disrupt intersectionality as a 'unified' solution. If we are not careful, the seduction of intersectionality as a solution to confront unified, homogeneous constructions becomes a prior, unified solution in itself. Intersectionality becomes victim to the very phenomenon it seeks to undo. My argument is that in the primary task of dismantling borders between race, class, gender, age, sexuality and (dis)ability, intersectionality performs the solution as the unavailability of a unified solution. Derrida summarizes the predicament: 'You see, pure unity or pure multiplicity – when there is only totality or unity and when there is only multiplicity or disassociation – is a synonym of death' (Derrida & Caputo, 1997: 13).

Intersectionality: a theory about borders

I want to think of my subjectivity, identity and encounters as a Black lesbian feminist in terms of a psychic territory, picking up on Radhakrishnan's comment that 'Locations are as factual as they are imaginary and imagined, as physical as they are psychic, and as open to direct experience as they are to empathic participation' (Radhakrishnan, 2000: 56). The notion of a psychic location, where multi-layered experiences and emotional responses to those experiences intersect, brings to life the idea that 'The politics of location is productive ... because it makes one location vulnerable to the claims of another and enables multiple contested readings of the one reality from a variety of locations and positions' (Radhakrishnan, 2000: 56–7). The various locations within my psychic territory actively resist the vulnerability of multiple, intersecting claims. My theoretical, empathic participation in the articulation and politics of intersectionality is not always welcomed into the location of my emotional experience, particularly when it concerns multi-layered realities of oppression.

I re-read Crenshaw's (1989) theory of intersectionality as a theory about borders. When Crenshaw speaks of *Demarginalizing the Intersection of Race and Sex* ..., the 'demarginalizing' involves the actual, sociological margins, and the position and experience of being on the margins. Crenshaw explains that '[t]hese problems of exclusion cannot be solved simply by including Black women within an already established analytical structure' (Crenshaw, 1989: 140). In other words, saying 'Come on over the border, we include you' is not enough, as this does not move the border one jot; to do this is simply to be re-positioned across an existing border. Border plus border plus border plus border equates to borders in the plural. In stark contrast, the intersection of borders is greater because it accounts for the structural and emotional collision of the traffic of discrimination flowing in multiple directions:

> The point is that Black women can experience discrimination in any number of ways and that the contradiction arises from our assumptions that their claims of exclusion must be unidirectional. Consider an analogy to traffic in an intersection, coming and going in all four directions. Discrimination, like traffic through an intersection, may flow in one direction, and it may flow in another. If an accident happens in an intersection, it can be caused by cars traveling from any number of directions and, sometimes, from all of them. Similarly, if a Black woman is harmed because she is in the intersection, her injury could result from sex discrimination or race discrimination.
>
> (Crenshaw, 1989: 149)

In other words, what is required is an understanding of the injuries caused by the collision and why the force of the impact of the collision is so powerful.

This is not just an intellectual exercise; the injuries caused by the collision have an emotional impact. The problem is that acknowledgement of the injuries is both desired and resisted at the same time. Indeed, Crenshaw is clear that not to understand the collision at the intersection, and not to understand the ways in which the vectors of oppressive constructs play host and guest to each other across constructed borders, serve to produce, mask, censor and regulate the injurious impact with the following consequences: 'Black women are caught between ideological and political currents that combine first to create and then to bury Black women's experiences' (Crenshaw, 1989: 160). Awareness that I get caught up in, and collude with, the burying of my own experiences in order to avoid the emotional impact of multiple injuries is particularly excruciating.

The actual construction of borders further complicates the situation. Thiongo states that:

> ... if a border marks the outer edge of one region, it also marks the beginning of the next region. As the marker of an end, it also functions as the marker of a beginning. Without the end of one region, there can be no beginning of another. Depending on our starting point, the border is both

the beginning and the outer edge. Each space is beyond the boundary of the other. The border in between serves as both the inner and the outer of the other. It is thus at once the boundary and a shared space.

(Thiongo, 1996: 120)

The predicament of borders is thus: without the border, how can things be defined? But, at the same time, borders are indeterminable. Application of Thiongo's explanation to categories of experience becomes a question of trying to pinpoint the outer edge of, or marker of, a beginning and an end between race, gender, class, sexuality, age and (dis)ability. It would seem that, depending on our starting point, all categories of identity and experience are the beginning, end and outer edge; each category and experience is beyond the boundary of the other. Borders as a structure undo themselves. Borders produce a false binary. The structure of a border is an aporia, where aporia is the tension made up of, and arising out of, the 'impossible' or that which deconstructs itself in practice (Lesnik-Oberstein, 1994: 21).

In other words, the predicament is more than a paradox. In a paradox, the relationship and structure between the things in the paradox do not necessarily undo each other. However, borders simultaneously position and re-position; thus, position is undone. Derrida comments: 'That is what gives deconstruction its movement, that is, constantly to suspect, to criticize the given determinations' (Derrida & Caputo, 1997: 18). It is within the 'movement' of 'given determinations' that the 'possible' within the 'impossible' and the 'available' within the 'unavailable' can be found. The 'movement' of 'given determinations' of race, gender, class, age, sexuality and (dis)ability is a dynamic that is at the core of intersectionality, and a dynamic that is infinitely difficult to embody and feel.

The intersection or dissolution of borders between the constituent parts of myself and my experience is not just a difficult emotional task because I have the habit of thinking in bordered, categorical, hierarchical binaries; it is not just difficult because I have no patterns for relating across difference (Lorde, 1980a: 115); it is difficult because the construction of borders is contingent upon the 'impossible'. I rely on psychic borders for a delusion of emotional stability. This delusion is because the very structure of the concept of borders is inherently unstable. This instability becomes compounded by, is contingent upon and shares a similar inherent instability with the concept and conditions of hospitality.

Spivak states that '[t]he putative center welcomes selective inhabitants of the margin in order better to exclude the margin' (Spivak, 1979: 35). The question is: what do I allow in and what 'selective' criteria do I use 'in order to better exclude' to the margins of my consciousness? The criteria for 'selective inhabitants' to be allowed to cross, or not to cross, constructed borders have a direct bearing on intention, and vice-versa. Intention and construction are mutually constitutive and contingent. It would seem that both the intention and the construction of psychic borders, designed to exclude the unwanted to the margins, operate in the same ways, and for similar reasons, as socially constructed borders. The psychic and social intention is to disavow the anxiety of the 'unavailability of the solution'.

Intersectionality: the impossibility of hospitality

The tension is that, while I cannot 'afford to settle for one easy definition, one narrow individuation of self' (Lorde, 1996: 197) and 'realize that our place was the very house of difference rather [than] the security of any one particular difference' (Lorde, 1996: 197), this does not resolve the problem of absolute hospitality between the different selves in the 'bonehouse' (Mairs, 1989: 471) of difference. Derrida explains the problem:

> The law of hospitality, the express law that governs the general concept of hospitality, appears as a paradoxical law, pervertible or perverting ... absolute hospitality requires that I open up my home and that I give not only to the foreigner (provided with a family name, with the social status of being a foreigner, etc.), but to the absolute, unknown, anonymous other, and that I *give place* to them, that I let them come, that I let them arrive, and take place in the place I offer them, without asking of them either reciprocity (entering into a pact) or even their names.
>
> (Derrida, 2000: 25; emphasis in original)

Application of this explanation to intersectionality might read something like:

> Absolute hospitality requires that I open up my 'bonehouse' of difference and welcome not only those identifiable categories and experiences of difference with name and status (such as age, race, class, gender, sexuality and [dis]ability), but to those absolute, unknown, anonymous other collisions, injuries, permutations and experiences of difference. Absolute hospitality requires that I *give place* to them, that I let them come, that I let them arrive, and take place in the place I offer them without any conditions. It requires that I offer unconditional movement between:
> ... all the parts of who I am, openly, allowing power from particular sources of my living to flow back and forth freely through all my different selves, without the restrictions of externally imposed definition.
>
> (Lorde, 1980a: 120–1)

Derrida's definition of 'absolute hospitality' is much more than a friendly welcome across the border. The problem is that the moment I say, 'My place is your place', the demarcation between the host in 'place' and the guest in 'place' is immediately undone. 'My home is your home' is a giving up of my home and, in doing so, a giving up of my position of host in my home. 'I *give place* to them' (Derrida, 2000: 25; emphasis in original) is to give up any sense of emotional security in the place of my 'bonehouse' based on stable categories of identity.

Actually, the implications of Derrida's imperative go much further, as summarized by Westmoreland: 'This very welcoming opens up into a violence. Such violence turns the home inside out' (Westmoreland, 2008: 6). Hillis Miller explains it in the following way:

> A host is a guest, and a guest is a host. A host is a host. The relation of household master offering hospitality to a guest and the guest receiving it, of host and parasite in the original sense of "fellow guest," is inclosed within the word "host" itself.
>
> (Hillis Miller, 1979: 180)

Derrida explains the dialectic as:

> ... the *hôte* who receives (the host), the one who welcomes the invited or received *hôte* (the guest), the welcoming *hôte* who considers himself the owner of the place, is in truth a *hôte* received in his own home. He receives the hospitality that he offers *in* his own home; he receives it *from* his own home – which, in the end, does not belong to him. The *hôte* as host is a guest.
>
> (Derrida, 1999: 41; italics in original)

This precarious situation is familiar and recognized in relation to national, social, ideological and political borders.

However, I propose that this is precisely the situation in relation to borders of experience, identity and feeling in the psyche. The situation is an interruption of the self. The precarity is that 'absolute hospitality' deconstructs the border between host and guest. As Westmoreland explains, '[t]he conditions for such hospitality are both the conditions for its possibility and its impossibility' (Westmoreland, 2008: 4). Returning to Thiongo's (1996) observation, it would appear that the conditions of hospitality are 'at once the boundary and a shared space' (Thiongo, 1996: 120), where the unconditioned needs the conditioned because the conditioned is constitutive of the unconditioned.

Hospitality is a tricky term; Derrida indicates this in the use of 'pervertible or perverting'. The trickiness is in the word itself:

> ... the word "hospitality" carries its opposite within itself ... The word "hospitality" derives from the Latin *hospes*, which is formed from *hostis*, which originally meant a "stranger" and came to take on the meaning of the enemy or "hostile" stranger (*hostilis*), + *pets* (*potis*, *potes*, *potentia*), to have power. "Hospitality," the welcome extended to the guest, is a function of the power of the host to remain master of the premises.
>
> (Derrida & Caputo, 1997: 110; italics in original)

Thus, we have numerous intersecting predicaments producing a difficult basis for an unconditional welcome:

- potentially, we have a hostile stranger who turns out to be the enemy, a parasite with the power to take over the 'bonehouse';
- we have the host, defined by her position, to welcome the guest in to her 'bonehouse' and remain proprietor; yet, the moment she says, 'my "bonehouse" is your "bonehouse,"' her 'bonehouse' is no longer her own;
- we have Derrida's 'absolute hospitality', where host and guest 'both imply and exclude each other, simultaneously ... exclusion and inclusion are inseparable in the same moment' (Derrida, 2000: 81), and as such, 'absolute hospitality' performs 'the law without law' (Derrida, 2000: 83).

The 'pervertible or perverting' law of the hatch

I want to offer a re-reading of the hatch example used by Crenshaw (1989) in the light of Derrida's aporia of 'absolute hospitality' in order to demonstrate the 'paradoxical', 'pervertible or perverting' (Derrida, 2000: 25) law of hospitality at work. In the example of the hatch, Crenshaw asks us to:

> Imagine a basement which contains all people who are disadvantaged on the basis of race, sex, class, sexual preference, age and/or physical ability. These people are stacked – feet standing on shoulders – with those on the bottom being disadvantaged by the full array of factors, up to the very top, where the heads of all those disadvantaged by a singular factor brush up against the ceiling. Their ceiling is actually the floor above which only those who are *not* disadvantaged in any way reside. In efforts to correct some aspects of domination, those above the ceiling admit from the basement only those who can say that "but

for" the ceiling, they too would be in the upper room. A hatch is developed through which those placed immediately below can crawl. Yet this hatch is generally available only to those who – due to the singularity of their burden and their otherwise privileged position relative to those below – are in the position to crawl through. Those who are multiply-burdened are generally left below unless they can somehow pull themselves into the groups that are permitted to squeeze through the hatch.

(Crenshaw, 1989: 151–2; emphasis in original)

It is clear that the hatch is not opened up to the 'absolute, unknown, anonymous other' (Derrida, 2000: 25). Hospitality is conditional, producing the criteria for a 'pact' (Derrida, 2000: 25). The 'family name' (Derrida, 2000: 25) criterion becomes the 'but for' (Crenshaw, 1989: 151), and Derrida's (2000: 25) 'social status' criterion could be translated as 'those placed immediately below' (Crenshaw, 1989: 152) and 'the singularity of their burden' (Crenshaw, 1989: 152). Position becomes criteria and criteria dictate position in a gradient of spatial and ideological proximity contingent upon sameness. Following this logic, those who due to their 'otherwise privileged position relative to those below' and 'placed immediately below' the hatch are offered hospitality. The 'absolute, unknown, anonymous other' are 'told to wait in the unprotected margins until they can be absorbed into the broader, protected categories of race and sex' (Crenshaw, 1989: 152).

Crenshaw's analogy of the hatch provides an apposite framework to interrogate how hierarchies of oppression (McDonald & Coleman, 1999) function to maintain the positions of host and guest within the collective 'bonehouse' of feminism, and within the individual 'bonehouses' of ourselves as feminists. Lorde asks:

What woman is so enamoured of her own oppression that she cannot see her heelprint upon another woman's face? What women's terms of oppression have become precious and necessary to her as a ticket into the fold of the righteous, away from the cold winds of self-scrutiny?

(Lorde, 1981: 132)

Stamping on the face of an aspect of self or on an aspect of another woman's self is the 'terrible injustice' Lorde spoke about in her reply to Robinson, quoted at the beginning of this chapter. Enamoured identification with 'mutually exclusive ideologies or priorities' (Crenshaw, 1989: 152) that lets 'one piece of yourself be cancelled out by another' (Savren & Robinson, 1982: 81–2) produces false hierarchies of oppression.

Hostile strangers: Black women go around to the back door

I contend that it is possible to trace the 'paradoxical', 'pervertible or perverting' law of hospitality at work in all of the examples that Crenshaw (1989) uses, such as: Black women and rape (157); Black women and 'sex-based norms and expectations' (155); Black women and their Black communities (155); Black women and white communities (156); Black women and the Black political agenda, including 'the Black liberation movement' (156); 'Black liberationist agendas' (150). In every example that Crenshaw examines, Black women are either completely excluded or 'have to go around to the back door' (Crenshaw, 1989: 161). In these multiple examples of inhospitality, Black women are recognized as the 'absolute, unknown, anonymous other' and, as such, represent the '"hostile" stranger' (Derrida & Caputo, 1997: 110). In other words, the 'absolute unknown, anonymous other' of Black women becomes translated into a known category, albeit hostile. Black women come to represent the situation whereby 'the foreigner lives within us ... the hidden face of our identity, the space that wrecks our abode' (Kristeva, 1991: 1). Lorde addresses this point in the following way: 'It's easier to deal with a poet, certainly a black woman poet, when you categorize her down, narrow her down so that she can fulfil your expectations, so she's socially acceptable and not too disturbing, nor too discordant' (Tate, 1982: 88). Ahmed summarizes the 'pervertible' machinations of the stranger situation as:

> ... we recognise somebody *as a stranger*, rather than simply failing to recognise them ... Strangers are not simply those who are not known in this dwelling, but those who are, in their very proximity, *already recognised as not belonging*, as being out of place. Such a recognition of those who are out of place allows both the demarcation and enforcement of the boundaries of "this place", as where "we" dwell.
>
> (Ahmed, 2000: 21–2; emphasis in original)

I would say that racism, sexism, homophobia, ageism, classism and (dis) ability discrimination are no stranger to me. Indeed, I make it my business to know and to recognize these forms of oppression. Intersectionality continues to focus my recognition so that I see the proximity between different forms of oppression with increasing clarity, and realize that they are rather intimate. However, in 'this place' of my 'bonehouse', I find that that which is no stranger to me becomes a stranger, and I become a stranger to myself.

The inward disturbance of intersectionality

The 'pervertible or perverting' characteristic of hospitality, and the 'pervertible or perverting' characteristic of borders, are constituted and function in similar ways. Hospitality and borders share a quality of internal instability; they supplement each other and function as supplements in their own right. Furthermore, it is becoming apparent that the 'pervertible or perverting' 'operates normatively; and how its normativity is rendered oblique almost to the point of invisibility' (Brown, 2008: 4).

The relevance to my argument of tracking how 'pervertible or perverting' operates, and the disavowal of its anxiety provoking machinations, is that this is at work in my 'bonehouse' of difference. It is the crux of the emotional difficulty I encounter in attempting to allow the collision of intersecting experiences and analyses of my different selves. Caputo explains:

> Derrida likes to say that we do not know what hospitality is, not because the idea is built around a difficult conceptual riddle, but because, in the end, hospitality is not a matter of objective knowledge, but belongs to another order all together, beyond knowledge, an enigmatic "experience" in which I set out for the stranger, for the other, for the unknown, where I cannot go.
>
> (Derrida & Caputo, 1997: 112)

Without careful scrutiny, the limits of hospitality could limit the availability of my fullest concentration of energy for the activism of Black feminist theory, and limit 'the transformation of silence into language and action' (Lorde, 1977: 40). However, as Caputo explains:

> Derrida's interest in exploring the tensions within "hospitality" is not aimed at cynically unmasking it as just more mastery and power … hospitality is inhabited from within, inwardly disturbed by these tensions, but he does this precisely in order to open hospitality up, to keep it on guard against itself, on the *qui vive*, to open – to push – it *beyond* itself. For it is only that internal tension and instability that keeps the idea of hospitality alive, open, loose.
>
> (Derrida & Caputo, 1997: 112; emphasis in original)

The emotional task of inhabiting intersectionality from within is residing with the inward disturbance.

Intersectionality: the foreigner

Derrida (2000) opens *Of Hospitality* with the 'Foreigner Question', formulated in the following way: 'As though the foreigner were being-in-question, the very question of being-in-question, the question-being or being-in-question of the question' (Derrida, 2000: 3). A close re-reading of Crenshaw's (1989) paper through Derrida's 'Foreigner Question' reads the intersectional experience of Black women's multiple oppression as 'the very question of being-in-question'. '[T]he very question of being-in-question' is at the heart of the 'psychological toll' (The Combahee River Collective, 1977: 266) of dealing with the foreigner within me. Both the intersectional experience and the foreigner are responded to in similar ways for similar reasons. The denial, exclusion and rejection of the intersectional experience are contingent upon logics that are used to deny, exclude and reject the foreigner. Both the foreigner and the intersectional experience of Black women seek recognition for admission through ideological, geo-political, physical and emotional border control.

Both the foreigner and the intersectional experience of Black women find themselves subject to the laws, questions and anxieties that determine border control. Westmoreland outlines the position and function of the foreigner:

> An individual was recognized by how he appeared before the law, what status he held in the *polis*. The foreigner was placed inside the law, under the law, essential to the law. The foreigner occupied an integral space within the city. Indeed, the foreigner was essential because he provided that to which citizens could compare themselves. From a phenomenological standpoint, one could claim that one's identity is only understood in relation to others. Citizens understand themselves in relation to others, to foreigners. "We are not those sorts of people. We are citizens." In the laws of hospitality, we find a multiplicity involving differentiation according to the right of the state. The state establishes rules through which people can be divided into citizens and non-citizens, citizens and foreigners, hosts and guests. It can identify individuals; and therefore, it can include or exclude whosoever it chooses based on the laws, which it has created.
>
> (Westmoreland, 2008: 2; italics in original)

Crenshaw (1989) demonstrates that the criteria, rules and laws invoked to exclude Black women's intersectional experience are contingent upon what is understood in relation to others. The key point is that these 'others' are known others: others that can be recognized and identified with. The foreigner is both constituted and situated by laws that demarcate what is to be included and excluded, 'predicated on a discrete set of experiences' (Crenshaw, 1989: 140). Crenshaw shows that, in the case of Black women's intersectional experience, the discreet is 'defined respectively by white women's and Black men's experiences' (Crenshaw, 1989: 143), thus, 'limiting inquiry to the experiences of otherwise-privileged members of the group' (Crenshaw, 1989: 140).

Pandora's box

When Black women 'placed inside the law, under the law, essential to the law' (Westmoreland, 2008: 2) presented their case of intersectional discrimination, the conclusion of the court was that:

> Title VII does not indicate that the goal of the statute was to create a new classification of "black women" … The prospect of the creation of new classes of protected minorities, governed only by the mathematical principles of permutation and combination, clearly raises the prospect of opening the hackneyed Pandora's box.
>
> (Crenshaw, 1989: 142)

This fascinating summary incorporated the key elements used in immigration control designed to include and exclude selective inhabitants. Those elements include the notion of the creation of a 'new classification' defined in relation to a prior known, the use of mathematical principles and the anxiety of 'Pandora's box'.

Westmoreland's (2008) depiction of the citizen's evaluation of self in terms of the foreigner that 'We are not those sorts of people' (Westmoreland, 2008: 2) is exactly the response of the courts and is exactly where the courts missed the point. The point is that Black women were saying exactly that 'We are not those sorts of people'; they were saying, 'We are not white women and we are not Black men'. Actually, Black women were contesting the 'mathematical principles of permutation and combination' (Crenshaw, 1989: 142) used by the court to classify and recognize injustice. It is, as Derrida explains: 'Justice, if it has to do with the other … is always incalculable. You cannot calculate justice' (Derrida & Caputo, 1997: 17).

'Pandora's box' becomes translated into what Honig observes as the familiar response to the foreigner: 'Again and again, I find foreignness used in familiar ways, as a device that gives shape to or threatens existing political communities by marking negatively what "we" are not' (Honig, 2001: 2–3). The device becomes a mechanism to produce a number of interconnected phenomena simultaneously. The device of the foreigner produces the threat, legitimizes a prior established set of knowns to identify the threat and produces the '"we" are not' border criteria for what is recognized/included and unrecognized/excluded.

It is a set of intersecting productions I recognize performed in my psyche in response to 'the very question of being-in-question' (Derrida, 2000: 3).

Black women since Sojourner[4] Truth, in 'question of being-in-question, the question-being or being-in-question of the question' (Derrida, 2000: 3), continue to ask, 'Ain't I a Woman?' (Truth, 1851). Crenshaw explains:

> Unable to grasp the importance of Black women's intersectional experiences, not only courts, but feminist and civil rights thinkers as well have treated Black women in ways that deny both the unique compoundedness of their situation and the centrality of their experiences to the larger classes of women and Blacks. Black women are regarded either as too much like women or Blacks and the compounded nature of their experience is absorbed into the collective experiences of either group or as too different, in which case Black women's Blackness or femaleness sometimes has placed their needs and perspectives at the margin of the feminist and Black liberationist agendas.
>
> (Crenshaw, 1989: 150)

Black women: the 'absolute, unknown, anonymous other'

The technique of dealing with difference through the polarities of absorption and rejection is articulated by Lorde as 'pretending those differences are insurmountable barriers, or that they do not exist at all' (Lorde, 1980a: 115). Lorde dismantles the hypocrisy of the 'too different' (Crenshaw, 1989: 150) logic in the following way: 'As white women ignore their built-in privilege of whiteness and *define* woman in terms of their own experience alone, then women of Color become "other", the outsider whose experience and tradition is too "alien" to comprehend' (Lorde, 1980a: 117, emphasis in original). The effect of using the experience, subjectivity and identity of the 'already known' as a measure is to absent anything that is absent from the match. Lorde traces these absences and she observes:

> The literature of women of Color is seldom included in women's literature courses and almost never in other literature courses, nor in women's studies as a whole. All too often, the excuse given is that the literatures of women of Color can only be taught by Colored women, or that they are too difficult to understand, or that classes cannot "get into" them because they come out of experiences that are "too different."
>
> (Lorde, 1980a: 117)

Lorde goes on to expose the contradictions, instability and arbitrary nature of the criteria of 'too different' (Crenshaw, 1989: 150; Lorde, 1980a: 117), pointing out that those who see Black women's work as 'too different' 'seem to have no trouble at all teaching and reviewing work that comes out of the vastly different experiences of Shakespeare, Molière, Dostoyefsky, and Aristophanes' (Lorde, 1980a: 117). Although contemporary academic courses may now include 'the literatures of women of Color' so that the manifestation, function and production of 'too different' may have altered since 1980, I would contend that the principle of Lorde's argument remains relevant.

The 'Foreigner Question' of the 'question of being-in-question' (Derrida, 2000: 3) is performed in the interview between Lorde and Rich (Lorde, 1979d). They discuss the matter of documentation, in which Rich proposes documentation as a mechanism to aid a form of understanding based on a shared identification that, clearly, was absent. Documentation becomes, for Rich, a passport to understanding the foreign Other, whereas for Lorde, documentation represents a passport to misunderstanding:

> *Adrienne*: So if I ask for documentation, it's because I take seriously the spaces between us that difference has created, that racism has created. There are times when I simply cannot assume that I know what you know, unless you show me what you mean.
> *Audre*: But I'm used to associating a request for documentation as a questioning of my perceptions, an attempt to devalue what I'm in the process of discovering.
> *Adrienne*: It's not. Help me to perceive what you perceive. That's what I'm trying to say to you.
> *Audre*: But documentation does not help one perceive. At best it only analyzes the perception. At worst, it provides a screen by which to avoid concentrating on the core revelation ...
> (Lorde, 1979d: 104; italics in original)

Documentation functions as a foreigner device to make known that which is unknown, measured in terms of what is known. Derrida comments: 'if I decide because *I know*, within the limits of what *I know* and *know I must do*, then I am simply deploying a foreseeable program and there is no decision, no responsibility, no event' (Borradori, 2003: 118; emphasis in original). In an attempt to move beyond the criteria of what is known, Rich uses the following reasoning: 'There are times when I simply cannot assume that I know what you know, unless you show me what you mean' (Lorde, 1979d: 104). However, all that is established is that Rich cannot assume she knows, and her request for documentation as a mechanism to 'show me' immediately unravels any position of not knowing; or, rather, it presumes a stability of a knowing self that is in need of mere confirmation rather than transformation.

There are several intersecting issues occurring here; a key point is that the request comes from Rich and, thus, it is Rich who establishes the criteria. Furthermore, documentation is not neutral. The historical, political and social symbolic significance of documentation is racialized, and has been used to police all kinds of boundaries between people, communities and nations. I am reminded of Lorde's journal entry from her two-week trip to Russia in 1976, where she writes: 'I thought of the South African women in 1956 who demonstrated and died rather than carry passbooks' (Lorde, 1976: 29). Even though I was born and raised in Britain, I carry my British passport with me at all times, vigilant of the 'question of being-in-question, the question-being or being-in-question of the question' (Derrida, 2000: 3). Detailed deconstruction of the exchange between Lorde and Rich reveals the impossibility of 'the absolute, unknown, anonymous other' (Derrida, 2000: 25). Keating argues that 'No question to the stranger is pure because we already assimilate their being into terms that we can arrange into our own conceptions of being' (Keating, 2004: n.p.).

Conclusion

I conclude by using the theory of intersectionality to frame a possible re-reading of Lorde's description of the 'pellet of yellow coloring' (Lorde, 1978: 57) penetrating packets of margarine. Lorde remembers:

> During World War II, we bought sealed plastic packets of white, uncolored margarine, with a tiny, intense pellet of yellow coloring perched like a topaz just inside the clear skin of the bag. We would leave the margarine out for a while to soften, and then we would pinch the little pellet to break it inside the bag, releasing the rich yellowness into the soft pale mass of margarine. Then taking it carefully between our fingers, we would knead it gently back and forth, over and over, until the color had spread throughout the whole pound bag of margarine, thoroughly coloring it. I find the erotic such a kernel within myself. When released from its intense and constrained pellet, it flows through and colors my life with a kind of energy that heightens and sensitizes and strengthens all my experience.
>
> (Lorde, 1978: 57)

The sealed plastic packets of uncoloured margarine could represent the determined categories of identity that are bordered off by a range of mechanisms functioning to reduce Black women to one component.

The 'intense pellet of yellow coloring perched like a topaz' could represent the potential of the theory of intersectionality. The action of kneading 'it gently back and forth, over and over, until the color had spread throughout the whole pound bag of margarine, thoroughly coloring it', could be the toil of allowing different aspects of self to play host and guest to each other, so that host is guest and guest is host, breaching predetermined borders between categories of experience and identity. It is interesting to note that Anzaldúa (2007) also uses the metaphor of 'kneading' to embody the connection between aspects of identity. Anzaldúa states:

> I am an act of kneading, of uniting and joining that not only has produced both a creature of darkness and a creature of light, but also a creature that questions the definitions of light and dark and gives them new meanings.

> (Anzaldúa, 2007: 103)

The 'energy that heightens and sensitizes and strengthens all my experience' (Lorde, 1978: 57) could represent the productive potential – the possibility of transformation available in the impossibility of hospitality that constitutes the task of intersecting all of the different parts of myself.

This reflective analysis set out to examine the emotional turmoil of intersectionality. I argue that 'It's hard, it's very hard' (Savren & Robinson, 1982: 81) because the undecidable, aporetic space of intersectionality is a direct challenge to the propaganda of predetermined, 'tightly-drawn parameters' (Crenshaw, 1989: 152) that constitute identity positions in this racist, homophobic, patriarchal world. This propaganda operates according to an equation whereby certainty is synonymous with claims to rationality and order. Intersectionality is 'very hard' because it requires trust in 'our deepest and nonrational knowledge' (Lorde, 1978: 53).

I contend that the 'terrible injustice' (Savren & Robinson, 1982: 82) of being reduced to one component works in numerous ways. Firstly, the legitimacy of privileging one component of identity that functions to allow 'one piece of yourself [to] be cancelled out by another' (Savren & Robinson, 1982: 82) is contingent upon the criteria of an 'always already'.[5]

Second, the predetermined criteria of identity categories are a mechanism of regulation and control that limit the choices, resources and experiences of self-definition available to Black women. A predetermined decision is no decision at all. In stark contrast, the aporia of intersectionality enables a more just, responsible and ethical encounter with self and others. Unamuno explains that 'What I wish to establish is that uncertainty, doubt, perpetual wrestling with the mystery of our final destiny, mental despair, and the lack of any solid and stable dogmatic foundation, may be the basis of an ethic' (Unamuno, 2006: 230).

Third, the potential of the aporia of intersectionality moves beyond the self and forms the foundation for an ethical engagement with others. Butler explains how this works:

> If the subject is opaque to itself, not fully translucent and knowable to itself, it is not thereby licensed to do what it wants or to ignore its obligations to others ... Indeed, if it is precisely by virtue of one's relations to others that one is opaque to oneself, and if those relations to others are the venue for one's ethical responsibility, then it may well follow that it is precisely by virtue of the subject's opacity to itself that it incurs and sustains some of its most important ethical bonds.
>
> (Butler, 2005: 19–20)

The productive potential of the aporia of intersectionality is summarized succinctly by the Combahee River Collective: 'We believe that the most profound and potentially the most radical politics come directly out of our own identity' (The Combahee River Collective, 1977: 264).

Lorde cautions that '[w]e cannot settle for the pretenses of connections' (Lorde, 1983a: 153). The implications of this are infinite: an infinite referral and deferral of pretences of connections that form a complex web of interconnected pretences. Through the critical lens of aporia and intersectionality, I now understand that the 'pretenses' function to mask, censor and disavow the anxiety that connections within myself, with other Black women and across political alliances produce. The situation of remaining proprietor of my 'bonehouse' of difference is contingent upon the 'pretenses'.

The success of political coalitions, collaborative-working, alliances and bridge-building for liberation is dependent upon, and in direct correlation to, our, my and your capacity to be in the 'borderland' of self. Anzaldúa explains: 'A borderland is a vague and undetermined place created by the emotional residue of an unnatural boundary. It is in a constant state of transition. The prohibited and forbidden are its inhabitants' (Anzaldúa, 2007: 25). Being in the 'borderland' of self involves giving up inherited inhabitance of the habit of borders. Survival of the 'borderland' of self is not in that which is available, possible and known. So, to the question I am often asked and ask often of myself, 'If "*the master's tools will never dismantle the master's house*"' (Lorde, 1979a: 112; emphasis in original), and these are the only tools that I habit and inhabit, what and where are the alternative tools? My answer would now be 'the "absolute, unknown, anonymous other"' (Derrida, 2000: 25) within intersectionality in which 'our creativity can spark like a dialectic' (Lorde, 1979a: 111).

Notes

1 I use the word 'tolerate' with caution, aware of the aporia of tolerance and the relationship between tolerance, power and aversion, as superbly detailed by Brown (2008) and in the debate between Brown and Forst (DiBlasi & Holzhey, 2014). Lorde speaks of tolerance as 'the grossest reformism' (Lorde, 1979a: 111). For a more detailed exploration of the problematic of tolerance, please see Chapter 2: 'Black feminism is not white feminism in blackface'.
2 'The Combahee River Collective first met in 1974. During "second-wave" feminism, many black feminists felt that the Women's Liberation Movement was defined by and paid exclusive attention to white, middle-class women. The Combahee River Collective was a group of black feminists who wanted to clarify their place in the politics of feminism. The name of the Collective comes from the Combahee River Raid of June 1863, which was led by Harriet Tubman and freed hundreds of slaves. The 1970s black feminists commemorated a significant historical event and a black feminist leader by selecting this name' (Napikoski, n.d.).
3 'Rape Crisis (England and Wales) campaign continuously to raise awareness of the prevalence of sexual violence and, in particular, we highlight the importance and need for appropriate, high-quality and specialized support. Through our campaigns and briefings we raise awareness of sexual violence, challenge attitudes and press for change. We also work with other organizations, agencies and government departments to improve the response to those who are affected by and who perpetrate sexual violence. Rape Crisis Centres provide crucial crisis and long-term specialized counselling, support and independent advocacy for all women and girls of all ages who have experienced any form of sexual violence both recently and/or in the past; centres are community based, and independent of government and the criminal justice system' (Rape Crisis [England and Wales], 2004-2014).
4 Interestingly, 'Sojourner' is another word for 'traveller', which conjures connotations of the mobile foreigner.
5 The term 'always already' (Althusser, 1971) has been taken up by Black feminist scholars to communicate the predetermined categories of identity and positionality (Boyce Davies, 1994: 55; Chabram-Dernersesian, 2006: 185; Conboy et al., 1997: 3; duCille, 1994: 233; Durham, 2007: 10; Fulton, 2006: 11; Hammonds, 1995: 383; Hayes, 2010: 45; Shildrick & Price, 1998: 62; West, 1988: 32; Whelehan, 1995: 110).

5 Conclusion

'Where is the love?'

'See *too much*'

It could be said that this book has fallen into the dangerous trap of the dialectic explained by Žižek:

> The dialectical approach is usually perceived as trying to locate the phenomenon-to-be-analysed in the totality to which it belongs, to bring to light the wealth of its links to other things, and thus to break the spell of fetishizing abstraction: from a dialectical perspective, one should see not just the thing in front of oneself, but this thing as it is embedded in all the wealth of its concrete historical context. This, however, is the most dangerous trap to be avoided; for Hegel, the true problem is precisely the opposite one: the fact that, when we observe a thing, we see *too much* in it, we fall under the spell of the wealth of empirical detail which prevents us from clearly perceiving the notional determination which forms the core of the thing. The problem is thus not that of how to grasp the multiplicity of determinations, but rather of how to *abstract* from them, how to constrain our gaze and teach it to grasp only the notional determination.
>
> (Žižek, 2008a: x–xi; emphasis in original)

This book is structured around a number of interconnected aporia, tensions, problematics and predicaments. This book has endeavoured 'to break the spell of fetishizing abstraction' (Žižek, 2008a: x) in relation to issues such as positionality, the speech act, author function, representation, interstices, interdependency and borders by illuminating the links between these issues not only with each other, but also within the constitutive contexts that they inhabit. I have grasped at the 'multiplicity of determinations' (Žižek, 2008a: xi) to show the instability of determinations in order to contest any idea of 'an established' and to assert the undecidability of phenomena.

Furthermore, this book concerns, and uses, the methodological conceptual framework of Black feminist theory – a theory produced out of the dialectic of the suppression it seeks to resist. The suppression of Black women and their work is constituted of multiple and intersecting determinations reflected in, and resisted by, an immense range, breadth and depth of Black feminist scholarship.

This book has wanted to 'see *too much*' (Žižek, 2008a: xi; emphasis in original). What we see and do not see is highly political because 'an optics is a politics of positioning. Instruments of vision mediate standpoints' (Haraway, 1988: 288). I have wanted to see Black feminist standpoints that have been mediated out of the picture into the shadows and, then, judged accordingly. This is demonstrated in Christian's critique of the 1987 special issue of *Cultural Critique* entitled 'Minority Discourse', where even within a special issue foregrounding minoritized standpoints, the language used served to mediate these standpoints into the shadows. Christian explains that:

> ... the terms "minority" and "discourse" are located firmly in a Western dualistic or "binary" frame which sees the rest of the world as minor, and tries to convince the rest of the world that it is major, usually through force and then through language, even as it claims many of the ideas that we, its "historical" other, have known and spoken about for so long.
>
> (Christian, 1987: 14)

In addition, I have wanted to see how the production of 'The Occult of True Black Womanhood' (duCille, 1994) functions not to honour, but to demean Black feminist studies by 'treating it not like a discipline with a history and a body of rigorous scholarship and distinguished scholars underpinning it, but like an anybody-can-play pick-up game performed on a wide-open, untrammelled field' (duCille, 1994: 243).

I have emphasized the importance of context and welcomed the 'wealth of empirical detail' (Žižek, 2008a: xi) as an act of theoretical and narrative resistance (Beard, 2009) to confront the problem of the totalizing, 'always already', decided constructions of Black women and their lives. Indeed, this book is testimony to the 'multiplicity of determinations' (Žižek, 2008a: xi) about Black women that are deliberately absent and disavowed, and as such, the 'multiplicity of determinations' are much more than merely missing out a research variable. The variables are highly political. The 'multiplicity of determinations' that positions the scholarship of Lorde in particular, and Black feminist scholarship in general, is highly political. It is apparent that even though '[v]ariety, multiplicity, eroticism are difficult to control' (Christian, 1987: 19), this has not stopped those in domination from trying. Re-reading Lorde through a re-reading of contemporary and historical Black feminist writings and speeches from across the world has expanded and provided an important contribution to the understanding of the activism of Black feminist theory. This has been demonstrated through application of Black feminist theory, and Lorde in particular, to contemporary issues of Black feminist practice. The importance of this application is underscored by Christian, who says: 'I, for one, am tired of being asked to produce a black feminist literary theory as if I were a mechanical man. For I believe such theory is prescriptive – it ought to have some relationship to practice' (Christian, 1987: 13).

Resisting attacks on theory

In the current climate of negativity towards the value of theory, insistence on the positive value of theory is imperative. This book is a contribution to that insistence, and that insistence is politically charged because '[t]here can, of course, be no apolitical scholarship' (Mohanty, 1984: 19). I find Bion's psychoanalytic idea of 'attacks on linking' (Bion, 1959) particularly relevant to understanding the process of attacks on theory.

Eaton (2005) provides a detailed application of Bion's 'attacks on linking' to the notion of learning, and cites Bion's experiences of World War I as a critical context for the development of his ideas. Eaton comments that Bion 'realized that groups can become anti-learning assemblages and that failing to learn (indeed failing to think) can be a matter of life and death' (Eaton, 2005: 356). Keeping a grip of the capacity to think theoretically is 'a matter of life and death', and certainly, a matter of the life and death of the activism of Black feminist theory. Here, I am reminded of Christian's words: 'But what I write and how I write is done in order to save my own life. And I mean that literally … a way of knowing that I am not hallucinating' (Christian, 1987: 21).

Bion (1959) proposed that 'attacks on linking' between an idea (including the existence and structure of an idea), the understanding of an idea and the habitation of an idea within mental functioning are mounted by the psychotic parts of the personality, and can be found in borderline patients. Although Bion's (1959) psychoanalytic conceptual framework was developed in the context of working with borderline patients, and despite the problems of translating the clinical setting of psychoanalysis to the social setting (Parker, 2010), I think there is resonance with historical, liberal and current neoliberal attitudes and practices towards theory in general, and Black feminist theory in particular.

'Attacks on linking' has a number of relevant effects, including the attempted obliteration of mental functioning between, and within, the patient and analyst; the attempted destruction of the capacity to learn from experience;

and a 'nameless dread' (Bion, 1959, 1962, 1967) produced from a lack of containment of unbearable (beta elements) thoughts, feelings and imaginings that have been evacuated on account of the distress they cause. Eaton comments that:

> This word – *evacuated* – speaks to force and intensity. What is the fate of evacuated distress? Put more simply, what is the fate of the infant's cry of pain? In order for distress to be transformed, Bion suggests that it must find a home in the mind of another. Ideally a mind can be found to register the infant's pain. Still more important, that mind should belong to an individual more emotionally mature—someone with more experience of tolerating distress than the infant. If this is so, then pain can be more than registered, it can be recognized, reflected upon, and replied to creatively and compassionately. Bion asks the question: What does this other mind do for the infant in distress? Something helps the experience of raw emotional distress become an opportunity to evolve in the direction of discovering meaning. Bion says this something that helps is called "alpha function." The discovery of meaning depends upon the mother's ability to use her mind, including her attention, intuition, and emotional experience (all factors in her alpha function) to contain her infant's distress (the beta elements) and to transform that distress imaginatively.
>
> (Eaton, 2005: 358; emphasis and parentheses in original)

The raw emotional distress of being in a racist, homophobic patriarchy needs the rigour of theoretical containment in terms of recognition and processing of the distress. The cry of pain as a result of oppression needs to find meaning. Attacks on theory function to undermine the activism of all theory as a vehicle for resistance to oppression. In terms of Black feminist theory, it is an attack on the 'connection between experience and consciousness that shapes the everyday lives' (Collins, 2000: 24) of Black women and their work.

It could be argued that, just as Bion was interested from a psychoanalytic perspective in the condition and presentation of the borderline, this book shares this interest from a Black feminist perspective. The aporia of borders as a site of productive thinking is reiterated throughout this book both in terms of borders as a tool of regulation, and borders as an indeterminate space of subversive potential. This book set out to transgress temporal, spatial and disciplinary borders, and in the spirit of this intervention, I want to offer a re-reading of Anzaldúa's (2007) 'La Conciencia de la Mestiza: Towards a New Consciousness' through aspects of Bion's (1959) theoretical lens of 'Attacks on Linking'.

My purpose is to offer a particular application of Bion (1959) in order to insist on resistance to attacks on theory, and I believe that Anzaldúa (2007) offers such resistance. Anzaldúa states that '[t]he *mestiza's* dual or multiple personality is plagued by psychic restlessness' (Anzaldúa, 2007: 101; italics in original), and she explains that:

> In perceiving conflicting information and points of view, she is subjected to a swamping of her psychological borders. She has discovered that she can't hold concepts or ideas in rigid boundaries. The borders and walls that are supposed to keep the undesirable ideas out are entrenched habits and patterns of behavior; these habits and patterns are the enemy within. Rigidity means death. Only by remaining flexible is she able to stretch the psyche horizontally and vertically. *La mestiza* constantly has to shift out of habitual formations ...
>
> (Anzaldúa, 2007: 101; italics in original)

Although it could be argued that there are some similarities between Bion's and Anzaldúa's invocations of the borderline/la mestiza as overwhelmed by the flooding of 'undesirable ideas,' including the notion that the 'work takes place underground – subconsciously' (Anzaldúa, 2007: 101), a key difference in their formulations, as Anzaldúa describes, is that the 'struggle of the *mestiza* is above all a feminist one' (Anzaldúa, 2007: 106; italics in original). Although, here, Bion and Anzaldúa are concerned with the survival of mental functioning, Anzaldúa frames her political treatise in terms of unequal power relations in the context of a racist, homophobic patriarchy. In relation to surviving theory, I understand something of Bhabha's statement that: 'Survival, in that sense, is the precariousness of living on the borderline and has been one of my ways of close reading and writing' (Seshadri-Crooks, 2000b: 373).

'Attacks on linking' theory to activism stand in direct opposition to both the dialogical and dialectical foundations of Black feminist theory. I would argue that the following comment by Collins applies to all Black feminist theory: 'This dialectic of oppression and activism, the tension between the suppression of African-American women's ideas and our intellectual activism in the face of that suppression, constitutes the politics of U.S. Black feminist thought' (Collins, 2000: 3). Attacks on the activism of Black feminist theory are no coincidence or accident because '[o]ne key reason that standpoints of oppressed groups are suppressed is that self-defined standpoints can stimulate resistance' (Collins, 2000: 29).

Remaining steadfast in the insistence of the legitimacy and relevance of Black feminist theory is vital for social justice because 'As long as Black women's subordination within intersecting oppressions of race, class, gender, sexuality and nation persists, Black feminism as an activist response to that oppression will remain needed' (Collins, 2000: 22). This book contends that the activism of Lorde's theory in particular, and the activism of Black feminist theory in general, provide emotional, intellectual and spiritual containment for evacuated distress so that 'pain can be more than registered, it can be recognized, reflected upon, and replied to creatively and compassionately' (Eaton, 2005: 357). The activism of Black feminist theory in general, and Lorde's work in particular, produces a conduit to 'transform that distress imaginatively' (Eaton, 2005: 358).

Constrain our gaze?

I return to Žižek's point quoted earlier in this conclusion: 'The problem is thus not that of how to grasp the multiplicity of determinations, but rather of how to *abstract* from them, how to constrain our gaze and teach it to grasp only the notional determination' (Žižek, 2008a: xi; emphasis in original). Here in the conclusion, I want to attempt an abstraction in an effort to 'constrain our gaze' on 'the notional determination which forms the core of the thing' (Žižek, 2008a: xi), the 'thing' being the activism of Black feminist theory. Before I begin this abstraction, I want to make a number of points.

First, as much as I find the work of Žižek, Derrida and Foucault both affirmative in the task of articulating an emancipatory politics and refreshing in their audacity of imaginings of revolutionary grand theory, I would insist upon them, and other such like theorists, to answer the following questions: why do you not refer to Black feminist theory? Why is Lorde's revolutionary grand theory not in your writings, conference speeches and newspaper commentaries? Perhaps Žižek's comment that 'today, the false choice between "liberal democracy or Islamo-fascism" is sustained by the occlusion of radical-secular emancipatory politics' (Žižek, 2008b: 386) should be applied to the shameful 'occlusion' of Black feminist theory that is tantamount to an attack on linking.

Second, I would insist that they examine the principles of Black feminist theory and methodology, including:

- that Black feminist theory is constituted of the dialectic. In other words, Black women have formulated, crafted and communicated their theory out of, and because of, oppression (Collins, 2000);
- that Black feminist theory is constituted of the dialogical. In other words, Black women have formulated, crafted and communicated their theory out of, and because of, active engagement with struggles for social justice (Collins, 2000);

- that Black feminist theory is constituted of the erotic (Lorde, 1978). In other words, Black feminist theory goes beyond 'the encouraged mediocrity of our society' (Lorde, 1978: 54). Lorde speaks of the erotic as:

> ... a lens through which we scrutinize all aspects of our existence, forcing us to evaluate those aspects honestly in terms of their relative meaning within our lives. And this is a grave responsibility, projected from within each of us, not to settle for the convenient, the shoddy, the conventionally expected, nor the merely safe.
>
> (Lorde, 1978: 57)

Third, I would give voice to my own disquiet. If '*the master's tools will never dismantle the master's house*' (Lorde, 1979a: 112; emphasis in original), how do I reconcile using the conceptual frameworks of white men, such as Derrida and Foucault, to explicate the activism of Lorde's theory? Johnson comments that 'Jacques Derrida may sometimes see himself as *philosophically* positioned as a woman, but he is not *politically* positioned as a woman' (Johnson, 1989: 2; emphasis in original). Johnson's statement could be rephrased as the question: 'Can the "*philosophically* positioned" woman enable a theoretical understanding of the "*politically* positioned" woman?'

This book has demonstrated that the work of Derrida can enable us to understand that an aspect of '*the master's tools*' is the aporetics of positioning. Derrida does not provide an alternative to '*the master's tools*'; rather, his interest lies in how '*the master's house*' is constructed, including its architecture, foundations and supporting walls. I think the key is in '"working the cracks" ... by persistent use of her insider knowledge concerning its pressure points' (Collins, 2000: 282). Perhaps the process of forming different tools is in understanding how '*the master's tools*' function. For example, the reason why many Rape Crisis centres are constituted as collectives is based as much on knowledge and experience of hierarchical structures as it is on non-hierarchical structures. In other words, imperfect efforts to create alternatives to '*the master's tools*' are born out of knowledge of the function and results of '*the master's tools*'.

And, yet, my disquiet persists because the idea of using knowledge about '*the master's tools*' in order not to replicate these and, thereby, attempting the creation of alternative Black feminist inspired tools has a number of problems: first, it contains an inherent contradiction because any contingency based on an understanding of the function of '*the master's tools*' and a rejection of '*the master's tools*' is, in effect, using '*the master's tools*' to '*dismantle the master's house*'; second, '[t]he standpoints of the subjugated are not "innocent" positions' (Haraway, 1988: 286) and, as such, the idea that alternatives to '*the master's tools*' will naturally emanate from subjugated standpoints is flawed. Butler summarizes the essence of my disquiet:

> But I am writing here now: is it too late? Can this writing, can any writing, refuse the terms by which it is appropriated even as, to some extent, that very colonizing discourse enables or produces this stumbling block, this resistance? How do I relate the paradoxical situation of this dependency and refusal?
>
> (Butler, 1990: 121)

I agree with Collins that:

> Within these parameters, knowledge for knowledge's sake is not enough – Black feminist thought must both be tied to Black women's lived experiences and aim to better those experiences in some fashion. When such thought is sufficiently grounded in Black feminist practice, it reflects this dialogical relationship.
>
> (Collins, 2000: 31)

Thus, placing theoretical frameworks in a dialogue with the lived experience of grassroots Black feminist practice takes the 'activism' of Black feminist theory seriously. The multiple determinations that configure Black feminist scholarship within this book have been constrained into the 'notional abstractions' (Žižek, 2008a: xi) of applications to confront violence against women, and the necessity of Black-women-only reflective spaces and dedicated services. I hope that something of the essence of the conceptual frameworks used in this book can 'aim to better those experiences' (Collins, 2000: 31) of oppressed Black women.

However, in order to further demonstrate the potential, relevance and application of re-reading Lorde and Black feminist theory to current issues, I will conclude by pinpointing a number of issues alive in the Black feminist activism that I am presently engaged with. I propose that negotiating 'a channel between the "high theoretical" and the "suspicious of all theories"' (Boyce Davies, 1994: 43) can be achieved by exploring the relevance of theoretical frameworks in dialogical relation to the activism of Black feminist theory. Minh-ha summarizes the task as:

> ... a constant questioning of our relationship to knowledge, to way we reserve, transmit or bring it to bear on our daily activities. Our ongoing critical view of the system is motivated, not be a mere desire to blame, to right the wrongs and to oppose for opposition's sake. Rather, it is

motivated by the necessity to keep power and knowledge (ours and theirs) constantly in check for our own survival.

(Minh-ha, 2011: 125)

However, as a word of qualification, there is a difference between opening up a dialogue to show relevance and application, and the act of proving that a concept is correct by testing it against other concepts and practices. I find Bhabha's approach very useful:

> I set up a continual tension in the application of a concept, its translatability, and demonstrate at the same time its untranslatability. That's not to say its limits. A concept that merely shows its limits, or is pressed to do so, can still develop a sense of its ontological completion or authenticity – au fond, "this is what it really is."
>
> (Seshadri-Crooks, 2000b: 372)

With this caveat, here are a number of contentions alive in the Black feminist activism that I am presently engaged with that I have in mind.

Problem 1: paradox at the heart of feminism

> At what point, and in what ways, for example, does the specificity of a particular social experience become an expression of essentialism?
>
> (Brah, 1996: 95)

Trafford Rape Crisis in Manchester is an example of a service delivery model that has a dedicated Black, Asian and Minoritized Ethnic (BAME) women's helpline as part of a range of specific services for BAME women. The rationale for having this dedicated BAME service provision is based on recognition that the entrapments used to subjugate Black women – in this case, in the form of sexual violence – are different to the entrapments used to subjugate white women (Lorde, 1980a: 118). In other words, it is in recognition of the specific issues that BAME women face, and it is in recognition that the differences in the context, construction and constitution of sexual violence against Black and white women are 'differences that matter' (Ahmed, 1998). The BAME helpline service is advertised as a dedicated service for BAME women, so Trafford Rape Crisis assumes that the woman ringing the BAME helpline will be expecting the call to be answered by a BAME support worker. The dilemma is, for example, if the BAME helpline rings and there is not a BAME woman present to answer the call, should a non-BAME category woman answer the call? Is it better for the survivor of sexual violence, who is seeking support, to communicate and make a connection with another woman regardless of her racial category than not to have the phone answered at all?

Using the theoretical frameworks within this book, I am able to re-frame the operational issues presented by the BAME helpline in the following questions: what do the categories of 'Black' and 'white' function to do? Is there a danger here of privileging racial category above service provision? Indeed, is there a danger here of edging very close to the production of the authentic caller and authentic BAME support worker relation? What are the mechanics used in the invocation of the authentic? Does it matter who is speaking? (Foucault, 1969). Is the BAME helpline an example of the '*strategic* use of positivist essentialism'? (Spivak, 2006: 281; emphasis in original).

What I have come to know is that the problematic of how to balance the things women have in common with the differences between women is the 'paradox at the heart of feminism' (Spelman, 1988b: 3). Lorde elaborates the complexity of this paradox, stating that '[s]ometimes exploring our differences feels like marching out to war' (Lorde, 1983a: 165; Frye, 1983). The battle of developing a Black women's service within a feminist collective of Black and white women can, at times, feel overwhelming, and it is hard not to be seduced by the option of separatist solutions. However, Lorde reminds us of the value of the community of collective-working:

> As women, we have been taught either to ignore our differences, or to view them as causes for separation and suspicion rather than as forces for change. Without community there is no liberation, only the most vulnerable and temporary armistice between an individual and her oppression. But community must not mean a shedding of our differences, nor the pathetic pretense that these differences do not exist.
>
> (Lorde, 1979a: 112)

Problem 2: there is no atom

... there is no atom...

(Derrida, 1995, cited in Royle, 2003: 75)

Many of the women who use Rape Crisis helpline services use terms such as, 'I have others', 'inners' and 'alters' to refer to the different aspects of their internal world that speak. On the helpline, it is not uncommon for the identity of the caller to shift in the course of a call. The shift could be from an adult woman to a four-year-old child, and is frequently a shift to a different voice, gender, race, language, religion and belief system. The different voices hold alternative perspectives and information about the 'host' that often provide useful contexts or details about the trauma of the violence experienced; for example, the voices that emerge from the woman in witness protection when the 'host' is too frightened and too broken down to speak.

In the fifth edition of the *Diagnostic and Statistical Manual of Mental Disorders* (American Psychiatric Association, 2013) this is classified as a 'Dissociative Disorder', where 'Diagnostic criteria for 300.14 Dissociative Identity Disorder' are outlined as the following:

> A. The presence of two or more distinct identities or personality states (each with its own relatively enduring pattern of perceiving, relating to, and thinking about the environment and self).
> B. At least two of these identities or personality states recurrently take control of the person's behavior.
> C. Inability to recall important personal information that is too extensive to be explained by ordinary forgetfulness.
> D. The disturbance is not due to the direct physiological effects of a substance (e.g., blackouts or chaotic behaviour during Alcohol Intoxication) or a general medical condition (e.g., complex partial seizures). **Note:** In children, the symptoms are not attributable to imaginary playmates or other fantasy play.
>
> (American Psychiatric Association, 2013: 529; parentheses and emphasis in original)

Rape Crisis works with women from a feminist model based on the activism of feminist theory. The majority of women choose to use this service because the medical model has failed to understand, and assist with, the trauma of surviving sexual violence.

In feminist collective supervision meetings that function to explore the content and issues of the support work provided by Rape Crisis, I have found the theoretical frameworks used within this book of immense value. For example, Derrida's proposal that 'there is no atom' is explained by Royle in the following way: 'Everything is divisible. Unity, coherence, univocality are effects produced out of division and divisibility' (Royle, 2003: 26). This captures the essence of the multiple voices we encounter within a call on the helpline. Furthermore, the ways in which Black literary and oral narrative traditions of 'double-voiced texts' (Gates, Jr., 1988: xxv), polyvoice and polyrhythms (Boyce Davies, 1994: 23) have been taken up by Black feminists provide inspired approaches to conceptualizing 'a dialogue with the aspects of "otherness" within the self' (Henderson, 1989: 344).

The encounter with multiple voices within a call on the helpline disrupts the stability of the pronoun and, in the work of Rape Crisis, invokes the implications and tensions that constitute the politics of the pronoun that I pick up in this book in relation to Lorde's use of pronouns in the speech act (Austin, 1975; Barthes, 1967, 1971; Benveniste, 1961; Foucault, 1969). The ramifications of this interruption are demonstrated within analyses of the telephone call exchanges between Derrida and Cixous, which open up, and extend, the ways that the telephone functions as sightless voices of the indeterminate and multiplicitous other(s) (Derrida, 2006; Prenowitz, 2008; Setti, 2012). Reminiscent of these exchanges is a telephone call between Royle and Cixous (2012),[1] during which Cixous speaks about the telephone as an interruption of death and/or absence, an instrument of metamorphosis, and the tricks of time and delay that the answering machine introduces and offers. All of these characteristics and opportunities are present and put to use within the concept and practice of support that Rape Crisis helplines offer that is founded on the activism of feminist theory.

In addition, the notion of exceeding the bounds of the text (Barthes, 1967, 1971; Foucault, 1969) or, in this context, exceeding the bounds of voice and unity, and the concept of the supplement that 'is neither a presence nor an absence' (Derrida, 1997: 314), are further examples of theoretical frameworks within this book that have relevance within helpline support work. Moreover, the concept of the impossibility of hospitality, when applied to the situation of different voices inhabiting the caller on the helpline, disrupts notions of fixed positions of host and guest (Derrida, 2000). These are just some examples of theoretical frameworks that provide approaches to open up, rather than close down, the possibilities and productive thinking about the multiple voices that are present within a woman who uses Rape Crisis helpline services.

The work of Rape Crisis is about using voice (for example, through the helpline, writing, art, and therapeutic face-to-face and group work), enabling the specificity of women's experiences to be heard, and using this 'transformation of silence' (Lorde, 1977) to carve out emancipatory feminist intellectual, spiritual and emotional spaces. In many ways, this reflects the journey I am undertaking within the process of this book, where the move to coming to voice, being heard and, then, finding ways to make effective political use of voice is an ongoing and non-linear process. Collins expresses something similar in her journey of moving between the 1990 first edition and the 2000 second edition of writing *Black Feminist Thought: Knowledge, Consciousness, and the Politics of Empowerment*:

> I have learned much from revising the first edition of *Black Feminist Thought*. In particular, the subjective experience of writing the first edition in the mid-1980s and revising it now has been markedly different. I can remember how difficult it was for me to write the first edition.

Then my concerns centred on coming to voice, especially carving out the intellectual and political space that would enable me to be heard ... I am in another place now. I remain less preoccupied with coming to voice because I know how quickly voice can be taken away. My concern now lies in finding effective ways to use the voice that I have claimed while I have it.

(Collins, 2000: xii–xiii; italics in original)

Occupying the space of the concept

This book has a specific focus on the activism of Black feminist theory articulated through a re-reading of Lorde. However, the reach of its applications applies to the activism of all theory as liberatory practice (hooks, 1994). The task of inhabiting theory invokes a core theme of the book: namely, the aporetics of positionality. I find Bhabha's metaphorical use of habitation and occupation of theory, formulated in conversation with Seshadri-Crooks, particularly relevant here:

I like to think that the reader can almost be moved into occupying that space of the concept or the language and be placed in media res. I would almost like it to be a theatricalization of theory so that the reader is a part of it and does not understand it sitting in her chair overlooking and judging the concept from a distance.

(Seshadri-Crooks, 2000b: 372)

... an experience of how, in motion, in transition, in movement, you must continually build a habitation for your ideas, your thoughts, and yourself.

(Seshadri-Crooks, 2000b: 373)

Undertaking the objectives of the analysis in this book has involved 'continually build[ing] a habitation for' and 'occupying that space of the concept'. Nawal El Saadawi summarizes the difficulty of this occupancy: 'I create words but words create me. Words are all I possess, yet I am possessed by them ... Writing has been the antibook of death and yet, paradoxically, the reason why in June 1992 I was put on a death-list' (El Saadawi, 2009: 19). The aporia of to 'possess' and to be 'possessed', to 'create' and to be created and to be put on a 'death-list' because of the 'antibook of death' summons the aporia of the impossibility of hospitality.

In this conclusion, I want to pick up the theoretical lens of hospitality explored within the book in order to focus the gaze on the political imperative of theory. The issues of who is host and guest, constructing and deconstructing defences in relation to the 'absolute, unknown, anonymous other' (Derrida, 2000: 25) of concepts and maintaining a hospitable demeanour towards theory and the process of writing continue to be a challenge. The essence of the impossibility of hospitality is located in the dialectic of the position of 'the sister outsider'. Lorde's identification as 'the sister outsider' simultaneously encompasses the intimate proximity of 'sister' and the potential hostility of an 'outsider'. The situation of *hôte* (host) as guest and guest as *hôte* (Derrida, 1999), in terms of being simultaneously inside and outside of re-reading Lorde as host and guest in the activism of Black feminist theory, 'turns the home inside out' (Westmoreland, 2008: 6). Performing this in the context of neoliberal 'attacks on linking' within a racist, homophobic patriarchy amplifies the challenge. The task becomes the impossibility of hospitality of theory within a war zone.

The relevance of Kristeva's statement that 'a person of the twentieth century can exist honestly only as a foreigner' (Kristeva, 1977: 286) applies to the twenty-first century and beyond. The temporal and spatial indeterminacies of her statement are encapsulated by her observation that '[w]riting is impossible without some kind of exile' (Kristeva, 1977: 298). The question of the foreigner becomes even more complicated when the very theory inhabited teaches that the demarcation between the hostile stranger and the friendly stranger is mutually constitutive. Thus, any notion of a correct (friendly) and incorrect (hostile) reading or application of a concept is an entrapment. In an interview with Seshadri-Crooks, Bhabha explains that 'theoretical correctness seems subtly to defeat the process of conceptual work, which must entertain the possibility that any particular body of thought, despite its ruling paradigms and metaphors, has no sovereign mastery of control over its enunciation (inscription or interpretation)' (Seshadri-Crooks, 2000b: 377; parentheses in original). The boundary event of this book has revealed that:

> ... the limits of thought or theory are always showing through other borders of historical, conceptual, and ethical possibility. Theoretical thinking teaches us the nontransparency of ideas, the radical indeterminacy of signifying structures – and this must apply to the making and holding of theory itself, which demands a responsibility to the thinking of a problem as always in excess of, or in violation of, the tools for thinking it.
>
> (Seshadri-Crooks, 2000b: 377–8)

This book has responded to 'the radical indeterminacy of signifying structures' through finding 'the solution as the unavailability of a unified solution' (Spivak, 1985: 55). An excellent example of this is found in Derrida's 'turn from "guarding the question" – insisting on the priority of an unanswerable question' (Spivak, 1999: 425). Thus, rather than guarding the question of how and why 'Black feminism is not white feminism in blackface' (Lorde, 1979b: 60), the book prioritizes the 'question of *différance* … that which must be differed-deferred' (Spivak, 1999: 425; italics in original). Within this book, the 'other borders of historical, conceptual, and ethical possibility' (Seshadri-Crooks, 2000b: 377) are the 'historical, conceptual, and ethical' borders of the activism of Black 'sister outsider' theory. The excess is in the dialectic of the border as: 'both the beginning and the outer edge … both the inner and the outer of the other. It is thus at once a boundary and a shared space' (Thiongo, 1996: 120). The 'boundary event' (Minh-ha, 2011) of the activism of Black 'sister outsider' theory encapsulates the essence of the aporia. The event of the erotic (Lorde, 1978), both as the methodology and the subject under analysis within this book, 'opens up an interstitial space for the negotiation of meaning, value, judgment' (Seshadri-Crooks, 2000b: 376).

Where is the love?

There is nothing sentimental about Jordan's (1978) question, 'Where is the love?' This question structures Jordan's analysis of a public seminar entitled 'Feminism and the Black Woman Writer', at the 1978 National Black Writer's Conference in Howard University. Jordan states:

> From phone calls and other kinds of gossip, I knew that the very scheduling of this seminar had managed to divide people into camps prepared for war. Folks were so jumpy, in fact, that when I walked into the theatre I ran into several Black feminists and then several Black men who, I suppose, just to be safe, had decided not to speak to anyone outside the immediate circle of supportive friends they had brought with them. The session was going to be hot.
>
> (Jordan, 1978: 82)

It reminds me of the battles that take place behind the scenes of every event that speaks out about the activism of Black feminist theory that I know of.

Out of all of the battles, including practicalities such as funding, accommodation, venue, bureaucracy and time, by far the most arduous is often that of the battle for the legitimate right to the audacity to insist on the intellectual, emotional and spiritual space of the activism of Black feminist theory. However, Black women know in their gut that 'in politics, "major repercussions" do not come by themselves: true, one has to lay the groundwork for them by means of patient work, but one should also know to seize the moment when it arrives' (Žižek, 2008b: 392). In terms of tactics for negotiating a channel between a resolute insistence that spaces for the activism of Black feminist theory must be imagined and made available, and succumbing to criticism and doubt, I understand something of Jordan's predicament:

> I wanted to see if it was possible to say things that people believe they don't want to hear, without having to kick ass and without looking the fool for holding out your hand. Was there some way to say, to insist on, each, perhaps disagreeable, individual orientation and nonetheless leave the union of Black men and Black women, as a people, intact? I felt there had to be …
>
> (Jordan, 1978: 83)

In answer to the question of, 'Where is the love?', I know that this comes from colleagues, friends and 'sister outsiders', but primarily, it comes from contemporary and historical Black feminist texts and speeches providing testimony that the journey of creating/events/spaces of the activism of Black feminist theory was well-trodden. For example, in her 1974 address at the conference on 'Black Women in America', Chisholm declared:

> And I stand here tonight to tell to you, my sisters, that if you have the courage of your convictions, you must stand up and be counted … Forget traditions! Forget conventionalisms! Forget what the world will say whether you're *in* your place or *out* of your place. [Applause.] Stand up and be counted. Do *your* thing …
>
> (Chisholm, 1974: 137; emphasis and parentheses in original)

And, of course, the relevance of the question 'Where is the love?' is enduring. 'Where is the love?' underlies the day-to-day realities of the activism of Black feminist theory. 'Where is the love?' structures 'the priority of an unanswerable question' (Spivak, 1999: 425) faced with a series of infinite referrals and deferrals manifest in: do we stay at home to put our children to bed, to have time with them after they have been in the cruel world, or do we go to the feminist collective political meeting? Do we stay at home to hold our children, partners, sisters, brothers and neighbours, and contain their anxieties and their need to be held, in every sense of the word, or do we do our shift on the helpline to hold and contain the women who have been raped, battered and tortured? Do we give our Black sister a lift home or do we let her take two buses across Greater Manchester in the dark and cold on her own because we are too exhausted, because we have a deadline and/or because we need to get home? After all, it is 11pm and we left the house at 7am, leaving our children at breakfast club. 'Where is the love?'

I conclude with words from Jordan that constitute the work of this book and the work to be done:

> As a Black woman/feminist, I must look about me, with trembling, and with shocked anger, at the endless waste, the endless suffocation of my sisters: the bitter sufferings of hundreds of thousands of women who are the sole parents, the mothers of hundreds of thousands of children, the desolation and the futility of women trapped by demeaning, lowest-paying occupations, the unemployed, the bullied, the beaten, the battered, the ridiculed, the slandered, the trivialized, the raped, and the sterilized, the lost millions and multimillions of beautiful, creative, and momentous lives turned to ashes on the pyre of gender identity. I must look about me and, as a Black feminist, I must ask myself: *Where is the love?* How is my own lifework serving to end these tyrannies, these corrosions of sacred possibility?
>
> (Jordan, 1978: 85–6; emphasis in original)

Note

1 You can hear the telephone conversation between Royle and Cixous (2012) at http://www.sussex.ac.uk/video/schools/english/HeleneCixousOnTheTelephone.mp3 and a transcript of the call is at http://gullsofbrighton.wordpress.com/2011/06/09/distance-and-intimacy-cixous-on-the-telephone/#more-110 (Gulls of Brighton, 2011).

References

Abod, J. (1987) 'Audre Lorde: A Radio Profile'. *In* Wylie Hall, J. (ed.) (2004) *Conversations with Audre Lorde.* Jackson: University Press of Mississippi, pp. 158–63.

Ahmed, S. (1998) *Differences That Matter: Feminist Theory and Postmodernism.* Cambridge: Cambridge University Press.

Ahmed, S. (2000) *Strange Encounters: Embodied Others in Post-Coloniality.* London: Routledge.

Ahmed, S. (2004) *The Cultural Politics of Emotion.* London: Routledge.

Ahmed, S. (2009) 'Embodying diversity: problems and paradoxes for Black feminists'. *Race, Ethnicity and Education*, 12 (1) March: 41–52.

Ahmed, S. (2010) *The Promise of Happiness.* Durham, NC: Duke University Press.

Ahmed, S. (2012) *On Being Included: Racism and Diversity in Institutional Life.* Durham, NC: Duke University Press.

Ahmed, S. (no date) *feministkilljoys: killing joy as a world making project.* [Online] [Accessed on 27th December, 2013] http://feministkilljoys.com/

Alarcón, N. (1990) 'The Theoretical Subject(s) of This Bridge Called My Back and Anglo-American Feminism.' *In* Anzaldúa, G. (ed.) (1990) *Making Face, Making Soul/Haciendo Caras: Creative and Critical Perspectives by Women of Color.* San Francisco: Aunt Lute Books, pp. 356–69.

Alcoff, L.M. (1999) 'Toward a Phenomenology of Racial Embodiment'. *Radical Philosophy: A Journal of Socialist and Feminist Philosophy*, 95, May/June: 15–26.

Althusser, L. (1971) 'Ideology Interpellates Individuals as Subjects.' *In* du Gay, P., Evans, J. and Redman, P. (eds) (2000) *Identity: A Reader.* London: Sage Publications Ltd., pp. 31–8.

American Psychiatric Association (2013) *Diagnostic and Statistical Manual of Mental Disorders, Fifth Edition (DSM-5).* Arlington, TX: American Psychiatric Publishing.

Amos, V. and Parmar, P. (1984) 'Challenging Imperial Feminism'. *Feminist Review*, 17: 3–19.

Anthias, F. and Yuval-Davis, N. (1993) *Racialized Boundaries: Race, Nation, Gender, Colour and Class and the Anti-Racist Struggle.* London: Routledge.

Anzaldúa, G. (2007) 'La Conciencia de la Mestiza: Towards a New Consciousness'. *In* Anzaldúa, G. (2007) *Borderlands/La Frontera: The New Mestiza.* 3rd edn., San Francisco, CA: Aunt Lute Books.

Ashcroft, B. (1994) 'Excess: Post-Colonialism and the Verandahs of Meaning'. *In* Tiffin, C. and Lawson, A. (eds) (1994) *De-Scribing Empire: Post-Colonialism and Textuality.* London: Routledge, pp. 33–44.

Ata Aidoo, A. (1991) 'That Capacious Topic: Gender Politics'. *In* Mariani, P. (ed.) (1991) *Critical Fictions: The Politics of Imaginative Writing.* Washington, DC: Bay Press, pp. 151–4.

Audre Lorde – The Berlin Years 1984 to 1992 (2012) [Documentary] Directed by Dagmar Schultz. New York: Third World Newsreel.

Austin, J.L. (1975) *How to Do Things with Words: The William James Lectures Delivered at Harvard University in 1955* (eds J.O. Urmson and M. Sbisà). 2nd edn., Oxford: Oxford University Press.

Back, L. and Solomos, J. (eds) (2000) *Theories of Race and Racism: A Reader.* London: Routledge.

Banton, M. (1998) *Racial Theories.* 2nd edn., Cambridge: Cambridge University Press.

Barthes, R. (1967) 'The Death of the Author'. *In* Barthes, R. (1977) *Image, Music, Text* (ed. and trans. S. Heath). London: Fontana Press, pp. 142–8.

Barthes, R. (1971) 'From Work to Text'. *In* Barthes, R. (1977) *Image, Music, Text* (ed. and trans. S. Heath). London: Fontana Press, pp. 155–64.

Beard, L.J. (2009) *Acts of Narrative Resistance: Women's Autobiographical Writings in the Americas.* USA: University of Virginia Press.

Beauvoir, S.d. (2010) *The Second Sex* (trans. C. Borde and S. Malovany-Chevallier). London: Vintage.

Benveniste, E. (1961) *Problems in General Linguistics.* Bloomington, IN: Indiana University Press.

Bhabha, H.K. (1986) 'Foreword to the 1986 Edition. Remembering Fanon: Self, Psyche and the Colonial Condition'. *In* Fanon, F. (2008) *Black Skin, White Masks* (trans. C.L. Markmann). London: Pluto Press, pp. xxi–xxxvii. [Originally published in 1952 by Éditions de Seuil]

Bhabha, H.K. (1994) *The Location of Culture.* London: Routledge.

Bion, W.R. (1959) 'Attacks on Linking'. *International Journal of Psycho-Analysis*, 40 (5–6): 308–15.

Bion, W.R. (1962) *Learning from Experience.* London: Karnac Books.

Bion, W.R. (1967) *Second Thoughts: Selected Papers on Psycho-Analysis.* London: Karnac Books.

Borradori, G. (2003) 'Autoimmunity: Real and Symbolic Suicides – A Dialogue with Jacques Derrida'. *In* Borradori, G. (ed.) (2003) *Philosophy in a Time of Terror: Dialogues with Jürgen Habermas and Jacques Derrida.* Chicago: The University of Chicago Press, pp. 85–136.

Boyce Davies, C. (1994) *Black Women, Writing and Identity: Migrations of the Subject.* London: Routledge.

Brah, A. (1996) *Cartographies of Diaspora: Contesting Identities.* Abingdon: Routledge.

Brah, A. and Phoenix, A. (2004) 'Ain't I a Woman? Revisiting Intersectionality'. *Journal of inetnational Women's Studies*, 5 (3) May 1, 2004: 75–87.

Brown, W. (2008) *Regulating Aversion: Tolerance in the Age of Identity and Empire*. Princeton, NJ: Princeton University Press.

Brownmiller, S. (1993) *Against Our Will: Men, Women and Rape*. New York: Ballantine Books.

Brownmiller, S. (1999) *In Our Time: Memoir of a Revolution*. New York: Dell Publishing.

Burke, S. (2008) *The Death and Return of the Author: Criticism and Subjectivity in Barthes, Foucault and Derrida*. 3rd edn., Edinburgh: Edinburgh University Press.

Burman, E. (2004) 'From Difference to Intersectionality: Challenges and Resources'. *European Journal of Psychotherapy, Counselling & Health*, 6 (4) December: 293–308.

Burman, E. (2005) 'Engendering Culture in Psychology'. *Theory & Psychology*, 15 (4): 527–48.

Burr, V. (1995) *An Introduction to Social Constructionism*. London: Routledge.

Butler, J. (1990) 'Imitation and Gender Insubordination'. *In* Salih, S. with Butler, J. (eds) (2004) *The Judith Butler Reader*. Oxford: Blackwell Publishing Ltd., pp. 119–37.

Butler, J. (1993a) *Bodies that Matter: On the Discursive Limits of 'Sex'*. New York: Routledge.

Butler, J. (1993b) 'Passing, Queering: Nella Larsen's Psychoanalytic Challenge'. *In* Abel, E., Christian, B. and Moglen, H. (eds) (1997) *Female Subjects in Black and White: Race, Psychoanalysis, Feminism*. Berkeley and Los Angeles: University of California Press, pp. 266–84.

Butler, J. (1997a) *The Psychic Life of Power: Theories in Subjection*. Stanford, CA: Stanford University Press.

Butler, J. (1997b) *Excitable Speech: A Politics of the Performative*. New York: Routledge.

Butler, J. (1999) 'Preface'. *In* Butler, J. (2006) *Gender Trouble: Feminism and the Subversion of Identity*. 3rd edn., New York: Routledge, pp. vii–xxxvi. [Originally published in 1990 by Routledge]

Butler, J. (2004) *Precarious Life: The Powers of Mourning and Violence*. London: Verso.

Butler, J. (2005) *Giving an Account of Oneself*. USA: Fordham University Press.

Butler, J. (2006) *Gender Trouble: Feminism and the Subversion of Identity*. 3rd edn., New York: Routledge.

Butler, J., Guillory, J. and Thomas, K. (eds) (2000) *What's Left of Theory?: New Work on the Politics of Literary Theory*. New York: Routledge.

Byrd, R.P. (2009) 'Introduction. Create Your Own Fire: Audre Lorde and the Tradition of Black Radical Thought'. *In* Byrd, R.P., Cole, J.B. and Guy-Sheftall, B. (eds) (2009) *I Am Your Sister: Collected and Unpublished Writings of Audre Lorde*. Oxford: Oxford University Press, pp. 3–36.

Byrd, R.P., Cole, J.B. and Guy-Sheftall, B. (eds) (2009) *I Am Your Sister: Collected and Unpublished Writings of Audre Lorde*. Oxford: Oxford University Press.

Carby, H.V. (1987) *Reconstructing Womanhood: The Emergence of the Afro-American Woman Novelist.* New York: Oxford University Press, Inc.

Caselli, D. (2005) *Beckett's Dantes: Intertextuality in the Fiction and Criticism.* Manchester: Manchester University Press.

Cashmore, E. and Jennings, J. (eds) (2001) *Racism: Essential Readings.* London: Sage Publications, Ltd.

Cavin, S. (1983) 'An Interview with Audre Lorde'. *In* Wylie Hall, J. (ed.) (2004) *Conversations with Audre Lorde.* Jackson, MI: University Press of Mississippi, pp. 101–8.

Chabram-Dernersesian, A. (ed.) (2006) *The Chicana/o Cultural Studies Reader.* New York: Routledge.

Chisholm, S. (1974) 'The Black Woman in Contemporary America'. *In* Daley, J. (ed.) (2006) *Great Speeches by African Americans: Frederick Douglass, Sojourner Truth, Dr. Martin Luther King, Jr., Barack Obama, and Others.* New York: Dover Publications, pp. 132–7.

Christian, B. (1987) 'The Race for Theory'. *In* James, J. and Sharpley-Whiting, T.D. (eds) (2000) *The Black Feminist Reader.* Oxford: Blackwell Publishers Ltd., pp. 11–23.

Christian, B. (1990) '"Somebody Forgot to Tell Somebody Something": African-American Women's Historical Novels.' *In* Bhavnani, K. (ed.) (2001) *Feminism and 'Race'.* Oxford: Oxford University Press, pp. 220–32.

Cole, E.R. (2009) 'Intersectionality and Research in Psychology'. *American Psychologist*, 64: s170–80.

Cole, J.B. (2009) 'Audre Lorde: My Shero, My Teacher, My Sister Friend'. *In* Byrd, R.P., Cole, J.B. and Guy-Sheftall, B. (eds) (2009) *I Am Your Sister: Collected and Unpublished Writings of Audre Lorde.* Oxford: Oxford University Press, pp. 231–7.

Collins, P.H. (1998) *Fighting Words: Black Women and the Search for Justice.* Minneapolis, MN: University of Minnesota Press.

Collins, P.H. (2000) *Black Feminist Thought: Knowledge, Consciousness, and the Politics of Empowerment.* 2nd edn., London: Routledge.

Conboy, K., Medina, N. and Stanbury, S. (eds) (1997) *Writing on the Body: Female Embodiment and Feminist Theory.* New York: Columbia University Press.

Crenshaw, K. (1989) 'Demarginalizing the Intersection of Race and Sex: A Black Feminist Critique of Antidiscrimination Doctrine, Feminist Theory and Antiracist Politics'. *The University of Chicago Legal Forum. Feminism in the Law: Theory, Practice and Criticism*, 1989: 139–67.

Crenshaw, K. (1991) 'Mapping the Margins: Intersectionality, Identity Politics, and Violence Against Women of Color'. *Stanford Law Review*, 43 (6): 1241–99.

Currie, M. (2004) *Difference.* London: Routledge.

Daly, M. (1978) *Gyn/Ecology: The Metaethics of Radical Feminism.* Boston, MA: Beacon Press.

Davis, A.Y. (1981) *Women, Race and Class.* New York: Vintage Books.

Davis, K. (2008) 'Intersectionality as Buzzword: A Sociology of Science Perspective on What Makes a Feminist Theory Successful'. *Feminist Theory*, 9 (1) April: 67–85.

De Veaux, A. (2004) *Warrior Poet: A Biography of Audre Lorde.* New York: W.W. Norton & Company, Inc.

Derrida, J. (1972) 'Signature Event Context'. *In* Derrida, J. (1988) *Limited Inc.* Evanston, IL: Northwestern University Press, pp. 1–24.

Derrida, J. (1977) 'Limited Inc. a b c …'. *In* Derrida, J. (1988) *Limited Inc.* Evanston, IL: Northwestern University Press, pp. 29–110.

Derrida, J. (1984) *Signéponge/Signsponge* (trans. R. Rand). New York: Columbia University Press.

Derrida, J. (1987) 'Envois'. *In* Derrida, J. (1987) *The Post Card: From Socrates to Freud and Beyond* (trans. A. Bass). Chicago: The University of Chicago Press, pp. 1–256.

Derrida, J. (1992a) *Acts of Literature* (ed. D. Attridge). London: Routledge.

Derrida, J. (1992b) *The Other Heading: Reflections on Today's Europe* (trans. P.A. Brault and M.B. Naas). Bloomington, IN: Indiana University Press.

Derrida, J. (1993) *Aporias* (trans. T. Dutoit). Stanford, CA: Stanford University Press.

Derrida, J. (1997) *Of Grammatology* (trans. G.C. Spivak). Corrected Edition, Baltimore, MD: The Johns Hopkins University Press.

Derrida, J. (1999) *Adieu to Emmanuel Lévinas* (trans. P.A. Brault and M.B. Naas). Stanford, CA: Stanford University Press.

Derrida, J. (2000) *Of Hospitality: Anne Dufourmantelle Invites Jacques Derrida to Respond* (trans. R. Bowlby). Stanford, CA: Stanford University Press.

Derrida, J. (2006) *H. C. for Life, That Is to Say …* Stanford, CA: Stanford University Press.

Derrida, J. (no date) 'Unsealing ("the old new language")' (trans. P. Kamuf). *In* Derrida, J. (1995) *Points … Interviews, 1974–1994* (ed. E. Weber). Stanford, CA: Stanford University Press, pp. 115–31.

Derrida, J. and Caputo, J.D. (1997) *Deconstruction in a Nutshell: A Conversation with Jacques Derrida* (ed. J.D. Caputo). New York: Fordham University Press.

Derrida, J. and Stiegler, B. (2002) *Echographies of Television* (trans. J. Bajorek). Cambridge: Polity Press.

DiBlasi, L. and Holzhey, C.F.E. (eds) (2014) *The Power of Tolerence: A Debate.* New York: Columbia University Press.

duCille, A. (1994) 'The Occult of True Black Womanhood: Critical Demeanor and Black Feminist Studies'. *In* Bhavnani, K. (ed.) (2001) *Feminism and 'Race'.* Oxford: Oxford University Press, pp. 233–60.

Durham, A.S. (2007) *Homegirl Going Home: Hip Hop Feminism and the Representational Politics of Location.* Illinois: ProQuest.

Eaton, J.L. (2005) 'The Obstructive Object'. *Psychoanalytic Review*, 92 (3) June: 354–72.

El Saadawi, N. (2009) *Walking through Fire: The Later Years of Nawal El Saadawi* (trans. S. Hetata). 2nd edn., London: Zed Books.

Evans, M. (1979) 'My Words Will Be There'. *In* Wylie Hall, J. (ed.) (2004) *Conversations with Audre Lorde.* Jackson, MS: University Press of Mississippi, pp. 71–8.

Fanon, F. (2008) *Black Skin, White Masks* (trans. C.L. Markmann). London: Pluto Press. [Originally published in 1952 by Éditions de Seuil]

Foucault, M. (1969) 'What Is an Author?' (trans. J.V. Harari). *In* Rabinow, P. (ed.) (1984) *The Foucault Reader: An Introduction to Foucault's Thought.* London: Penguin Books, pp. 101–20.

Foucault, M. (1975) *The Birth of the Clinic: An Archaeology of Medical Perception* (trans. A.M. Sheridan Smith). New York: Vintage.

Foucault, M. (1977) *Discipline and Punishment.* London: Allen Lane.

Foucault, M. (1981) 'The Order of Discourse'. *In* Young, R. (ed.) (1981) *Untying the Text: A Post-Structuralist Reader.* Boston: Routledge & Kegan Paul Ltd., pp. 48–78.

Foucault, M. (1982) 'The Subject and Power'. *In* Dreyfus, H.L. and Rabinow, P. (eds) (1993) *Michel Foucault: Beyond Structuralism and Hermeneutics.* 2nd edn., Chicago: University of Chicago Press, pp. 208–26.

Frye, M. (1983) *The Politics of Reality: Essays in Feminist Theory.* Berkeley: Crossing Press.

Fulton, D.S. (2006) *Speaking Power: Black Feminist Orality in Women's Narratives of Slavery.* Albany, NY: State University of New York Press.

Garland, C. (ed.) (1998) *Understanding Trauma: A Psychoanalytical Approach.* New York: Routledge.

Gates, H.L. (1986) 'Writing Race'. *In* Ashcroft, B., Griffiths, G. and Tiffin, H. (eds) (2006) *The Post-Colonial Studies Reader.* 2nd edn., London: Routledge, pp. 216–18.

Gates, H.L., Jr. (1988) *The Signifying Monkey: A Theory of African-American Literary Criticism.* New York: Oxford University Press.

Greene, L.A. (1989) 'Breaking the Barriers of Silence'. *In* Wylie Hall, J. (ed.) (2004) *Conversations with Audre Lorde.* Jackson, MS: University Press of Mississippi, pp. 181–3.

Grzanka, P. (ed.) (2014) *Intersectionality: A Foundations and Frontiers Reader.* Colorado: Westview Press.

Gulls of Brighton: A certain non-place. (2011) *Distance and Intimacy: Cixous on the Telephone.* [Online] [Accessed on 1st February, 2013] http://gullsofbrighton.wordpress.com/2011/06/09/distance-and-intimacy-cixous-on-the-telephone/#more-110

Gunaratnam, Y. (2003) *Researching Race and Ethnicity: Methods, Knowledge and Power.* London: Sage Publications, Ltd.

Guy-Sheftall, B. (2009) 'Epilogue. Bearing Witness: The Legacy of Audre Lorde'. *In* Byrd, R.P., Cole, J.B. and Guy-Sheftall, B. (eds) (2009) *I Am Your Sister: Collected and Unpublished Writings of Audre Lorde.* Oxford: Oxford University Press, pp. 253–60.

Hall, S. (1996) 'Who Needs "Identity"?' *In* du Gay, P., Evans, J. and Redman, P. (eds) (2000) *Identity: A Reader.* London: Sage Publications, pp. 15–30.

Hall, S. (ed.) (1997) *Representation: Cultural Representations and Signifying Practices.* London: Sage Publications, Ltd.

Hammonds, E. (1995) 'Black (W)holes and the Geometry of Black Female Sexuality'. *In* Bhavnani, K. (ed.) (2001) *Feminism and 'Race'.* Oxford: Oxford University Press, pp. 379–93.

Haraway, D. (1988) 'Situated Knowledges: The Science Question in Feminism and the Privilege of Partial Perspective'. *Feminist Studies*, 14 (3) Autumn: 575–99.

Harding, S. (1993) 'Rethinking Standpoint Epistemology: "What Is Strong Objectivity"?' *In* Alcoff, L. and Potter, E. (eds) (1993) *Feminist Epistemologies.* New York: Routledge, Chapman and Hall, Inc., pp. 49–82.

Hayes, E.M. (2010) *Songs in Black and Lavender: Race, Sexual Politics, and Women's Music.* Illinois: University of Illinois Press.

Henderson, M.G. (1989) 'Speaking in Tongues: Dialogics, Dialectics, and the Black Woman Writer's Literary Tradition'. *In* Smith, S. and Watson, J. (eds) (1998) *Women, Autobiography, Theory: A Reader.* Madison, WI: The University of Wisconsin Press, pp. 343–51.

Henwood, K., Griffin, C. and Phoenix, A. (eds) (1998) *Standpoints and Differences: Essays in the Practice of Feminist Psychology.* London: Sage Publications, Ltd.

Herman, J.L. (1997) *Trauma and Recovery: The Aftermath of Violence – From Domestic Abuse to Political Terror.* New Edition, New York: BasicBooks.

Hillis Miller, J. (1979) 'The Critic as Host'. *In* Bloom, H., de Man, P., Derrida, J., Hartman, G.H. and Hillis Miller, J. (2004) *Deconstruction and Criticism.* 2nd edn., London: Continuum, pp. 177–207.

HMSO (2000) *Race Relations (Amendment) Act 2000 (c. 34).* London: HMSO. [Online] [Accessed on 6th December, 2013] http://www.legislation.gov.uk/ukpga/2000/34/contents

HMSO (2006) *Equality Act 2006 (c. 3).* London: HMSO. [Online] [Accessed on 6th December, 2013] http://www.legislation.gov.uk/ukpga/2006/3/contents

HMSO (2010) *Equality Act 2010 (c. 15).* London: HMSO. [Online] [Accessed on 6th December, 2013] http://www.legislation.gov.uk/ukpga/2010/15/contents

Holzman, L. (2011) 'Critical Psychology, Philosophy and Social Therapy'. *Register of Social Critical Theories.* [Online] [Accessed on 17th November, 2013] http://loisholzman.org/wp-content/uploads/2011/01/Final.CriticalPsychPhiloST.pdf

Honig, B. (2001) *Democracy and the Foreigner.* Princeton, NJ: Princeton University Press.

Hook, D. (2005) *A Critical Psychology of the Postcolonial.* London: LSE Research Online. [Accessed on 17th November, 2013] http://eprints.lse.ac.uk/archive/00000950

Hook, D., Mkhize, N., Kiguwa, P., Collins, A., Burman, E. and Parker, I. (eds) (2004) *Critical Psychology.* Lansdowne: UCT Press.

hooks, b. (1982) *Ain't I a Woman: Black Women and Feminism.* London: Pluto Press.

hooks, b. (1984) *Feminist Theory: From Margin to Center.* Boston: South End Press.

hooks, b. (1989) *Talking Back: Thinking Feminist, Thinking Black.* Boston: South End Press.

hooks, b. and West, C. (1991) *Breaking Bread: Insurgent Black Intellectual Life.* Boston: South End Press.

Ingleby, D. (1985). 'Professionals as Socializers: The Psy Complex'. *Research in Law, Deviance and Social Control,* 7: 79–109.

Intersectionalities: A Global Journal of Social Work Analysis, Research, Polity, and Practice, 1, 2012 [Peer-reviewed, open-access journal, sponsored by Memorial University's School of Social Work] [Online] [Accessed on 4th March, 2013] http://journals.library.mun.ca/ojs/index.php/IJ

Johnson, B. (1989) *A World of Difference.* Baltimore, MD: The Johns Hopkins University Press.

Jordan, J. (1972) 'White English/Black English: The Politics of Translation'. *In* Jordan, J. (1989) *Moving Towards Home: Political Essays.* 3rd edn., London: Virago Press, Ltd., pp. 29–40.

Jordan, J. (1978) 'Where Is the Love?' *In* Jordan, J. (1989) *Moving Towards Home: Political Essays.* 3rd edn., London: Virago Press, Ltd., pp. 82–7.

Jordan, J. (1982) 'Problems of a Language in a Democratic State'. *In* Jordan, J. (1989) *Moving Towards Home: Political Essays.* 3rd edn., London: Virago Press, Ltd., pp. 126–34.

Joseph, G.I. (2009) 'Remembering Audre Lorde'. *In* Byrd, R.P., Cole, J.B. and Guy-Sheftall, B. (eds) (2009) *I Am Your Sister: Collected and Unpublished Writings of Audre Lorde.* Oxford: Oxford University Press, pp. 249–52.

Kanneh, K. (1992) 'Love, Mourning and Metaphor: Terms of Identity'. *In* Kemp, S. and Squires, J. (eds) (1997) *Feminisms.* Oxford: Oxford University Press, pp. 292–9.

Kaplan, C. (1994) 'The Politics of Location as Transnational Feminist Practice'. *In* Grewal, I. and Kaplan, C. (eds) (1994) *Scattered Hegemonies: Postmodernity and Transnational Feminist Practices.* Minneapolis, MN: University of Minnesota Press, pp. 137–52.

Keating, P. (2004) 'The Conditioning of the Unconditioned: Derrida and Kant'. *Borderlands*, 3 (1) [no page numbers] [Online] [Accessed on 7th March, 2013] http://www.borderlands.net.au/vol3no1_2004/keating_conditioning.htm

Keizer, A.R. (2004) *Black Subjects: Identity Formation in the Contemporary Narrative of Slavery.* USA: Cornell University Press.

Khanna, R. (2003) *Dark Continents: Psychoanalysis and Colonialism.* Durham, NC: Duke University Press.

Kraft, M. (1986) 'The Creative Use of Difference'. *In* Wylie Hall, J. (ed.) (2004) *Conversations with Audre Lorde.* Jackson, MS: University Press of Mississippi, pp. 146–53.

Kristeva, J. (1969) 'Word, Dialogue and Novel' (trans. A. Jardine, T. Gora and L.S. Roudiez). *In* Moi, T. (ed.) (1986) *The Kristeva Reader.* Oxford: Blackwell Publishers Ltd., pp. 34–61.

Kristeva, J. (1977) 'Why the United States'. *In* Moi, T. (ed.) (1986) *The Kristeva Reader.* Oxford: Blackwell Publishers Ltd., pp. 272–91.

Kristeva, J. (1982) *Powers of Horror: An Essay on Abjection* (trans. L.S. Roudiez). New York: Columbia University Press.

Kristeva, J. (1991) *Strangers to Ourselves* (trans. L.S. Roudiez). New York: Columbia University Press.

Krizsan, A., Skjeie, H. and Squires, J. (eds) (2012) *Institutionalizing Intersectionality: The Changing Nature of European Equality Regimes.* Basingstoke: Palgrave Macmillan.

Lesnick-Oberstein, K. (1994) *Children's Literature: Criticism and the Fictional Child.* Oxford: Clarendon Press.

Lévinas, E. (1969) *Totality and Infinity: An Essay on Exteriority* (trans. A. Lingis). Pittsburgh, PA: Duquesne University Press.

Lorde, A. (1976) 'Notes from a Trip to Russia'. *In* Lorde, A. (1984) *Sister Outsider: Essays and Speeches.* Trumansburg, NY: The Crossing Press, pp. 13–35.

Lorde, A. (1977) 'The Transformation of Silence into Language and Action'. *In* Lorde, A. (1984) *Sister Outsider: Essays and Speeches*. Trumansburg, NY: The Crossing Press, pp. 40–4.

Lorde, A. (1978) 'Uses of the Erotic: The Erotic as Power'. *In* Lorde, A. (1984) *Sister Outsider: Essays and Speeches*. Trumansburg, NY: The Crossing Press, pp. 53–9.

Lorde, A. (1979a) 'The Master's Tools Will Never Dismantle the Master's House'. *In* Lorde, A. (1984) *Sister Outsider: Essays and Speeches*. Trumansburg, NY: The Crossing Press, pp. 110–13.

Lorde, A. (1979b) 'Sexism: An American Disease in Blackface'. *In* Lorde, A. (1984) *Sister Outsider: Essays and Speeches*. Trumansburg, NY: The Crossing Press, pp. 60–5.

Lorde, A. (1979c) 'An Open Letter to Mary Daly'. *In* Lorde, A. (1984) *Sister Outsider: Essays and Speeches*. Trumansburg, NY: The Crossing Press, pp. 66–71.

Lorde, A. (1979d) 'An Interview: Audre Lorde and Adrienne Rich'. *In* Lorde, A. (1984) *Sister Outsider: Essays and Speeches*. Trumansburg, NY: The Crossing Press, pp. 81–109.

Lorde, A. (1980a) 'Age, Race, Class, and Sex: Women Redefining Difference'. *In* Lorde, A. (1984) *Sister Outsider: Essays and Speeches*. Trumansburg, NY: The Crossing Press, pp. 114–23.

Lorde, A. (1980b) *The Cancer Journals.* San Francisco, CA: Aunt Lute Books.

Lorde, A. (1981) 'The Uses of Anger: Women Responding to Racism'. *In* Lorde, A. (1984) *Sister Outsider: Essays and Speeches*. Trumansburg, NY: The Crossing Press, pp. 124–33.

Lorde, A. (1982) 'Learning from the 60s'. *In* Lorde, A. (1984) *Sister Outsider: Essays and Speeches*. Trumansburg, NY: The Crossing Press, pp. 134–44.

Lorde, A. (1983a) 'Eye to Eye: Black Women, Hatred and Anger'. *In* Lorde, A. (1984) *Sister Outsider: Essays and Speeches*. Trumansburg, NY: The Crossing Press, pp. 145–75.

Lorde, A. (1983b) 'There Is No Hierarchy of Oppression'. *In* Byrd, R.P., Cole, J.B. and Guy-Sheftall, B. (eds) (2009) *I Am Your Sister: Collected and Unpublished Writings of Audre Lorde.* Oxford: Oxford University Press, pp. 219–20.

Lorde, A. (1984) *Sister Outsider: Essays and Speeches.* Trumansburg, NY: The Crossing Press.

Lorde, A. (1988) 'A Burst of Light'. *In* Lorde, A. (1996) *The Audre Lorde Compendium: Essays, Speeches and Journals.* London: Pandora, pp. 235–335.

Lorde, A. (1996) *Zami: A New Spelling of My Name.* London: Pandora Press. [Originally published in 1982 by Persephone Press]

Lorde, A. (2000) *The Collected Poems of Audre Lorde.* New York: W.W.Norton & Company.

Lorde, A. (no date) 'Difference and Survival: An Address at Hunter College'. *In* Byrd, R.P., Cole, J.B. and Guy-Sheftall, B. (eds) (2009) *I Am Your Sister: Collected and Unpublished Writings of Audre Lorde.* Oxford: Oxford University Press, pp. 201–6. [Undated address, Box 8, Spelman College Archives]

Loring Brace, C. (2005) *'Race' Is a Four-Letter Word: The Genesis of the Concept.* New York: Oxford University Press, Inc.

Lott, E. (1993) *Love and Theft: Blackface Minstrelsy and the American Working Class.* New York: Oxford University Press.

Lutz, H., Herrera Vivar, M.T. and Supik, L. (eds) (2011) *Framing Intersectionality: Debates on a Multi-Faceted Concept in Gender Studies.* Farnham: Ashgate.

Mairs, N. (1989) 'The Way In'. *In* Smith, S. and Watson, J. (eds) (1998) *Women, Autobiography, Theory: A Reader.* Madison, WI: The University of Wisconsin Press, pp. 471–3.

Mbembe, A. (2001) 'The Intimacy of Tyranny'. *In* Ashcroft, B., Griffiths, G. and Tiffin, H. (eds) (2006) *The Post-Colonial Studies Reader.* 2nd edn., Abingdon: Routledge.

McCall, L. (2005) 'The Complexity of Intersectionality'. *Signs: Journal of Women in Culture and Society*, 30 (3) Spring: 1771–1800.

McDonald, P. and Coleman, M. (1999) 'Deconstructing Hierarchies of Oppression and Adopting a "Multiple Model" Approach to Anti-Oppressive Practice'. *Social Work Education*, 18 (1): 19–33.

Mens-Verhulst, J. van and Radtke, L. (2006) *Intersectionality and Health Care: Support for the Diversity Turn in Research and Practice.* [Online] [Accessed on 29th December, 2013] http://www.vanmens.info/verhulst/en/wp-content/Intersectionality%20and%20Health%20Care-%20january%202006.pdf

Mens-Verhulst, J. van and Radtke, L. (2008) *Intersectionality and Mental Health: A Case Study.* [Online] [Accessed on 29th December, 2013] http://www.vanmens.info/verhulst/en/wp-content/INTERSECTIONALITY%20AND%20MENTAL%20HEALTH2.pdf

Minh-ha, T.T. (1991) *When the Moon Waxes Red: Representation, Gender and Cultural Politics.* New York: Routledge.

Minh-ha, T.T. (2011) *Elsewhere, Within Here: Immigration, Refugeeism and the Boundary Event.* New York: Routledge.

Mirza, H.S. (ed.) (1997) *Black British Feminism: A Reader.* London: Routledge.

Mohanty, C.T. (1984) 'Under Western Eyes: Feminist Scholarship and Colonial Discourses'. *In* Mohanty, C.T. (2003) *Feminism without Borders: Decolonizing Theory, Practicing Solidarity.* Durham, NC: Duke University Press, pp. 17–42.

Mohr, C. (2013) *Contemporary Poetry. Audre Lorde.* [Online] [Accessed on 29th January, 2013] http://copos13.umwblogs.org/2013/01/16/audre-lorde/

Molz, J.G. and Gibson, S. (eds) (2007) *Mobilizing Hospitality: The Ethics of Social Relations in a Mobile World.* Aldershot: Ashgate Publishing, Ltd.

Morris, D., Morris, A. and Sigafoos, J. (2013) *The Impact of the Equality Act 2010 on Charities.* University of Liverpool: Charity Law & Policy Unit.

Morrison, T. (1983) 'Recitatif'. *In* Baraka, A. and Baraka, A. (eds) (1983) *Confirmation: An Anthology of African American Women.* New York: Morrow, pp. 243–61.

Morrison, T. (1987) *Beloved.* Great Britain: Chatto & Windus.

Morrison, T. (1992) *Playing in the Dark: Whiteness and the Literary Imagination.* Cambridge, MA: Harvard University Press.

Mukherjee, A.P. (1990) 'Whose Post-Colonialism and Whose Postmodernism?' *World Literature Written in English*, 30 (2): 1–9.

Napikoski, L. (no date) *Women's History. Combahee River Collective: Black Feminism in the 1970s.* About.com [Online] [Accessed on 16th August, 2012] http://womenshistory.about.com/od/timelines19501999/a/combahee_river.htm

Nash, J. (2008) 'Re-thinking Intersectionality'. *Feminist Review*, 89: 1–15.

Nayak, S. (2013) 'The Activism of Black Feminist Theory in Confronting Violence Against Women: Interconnections, Politics and Practice'. *In* Testoni, I., Wieser, M., Groterath, A. and Guglielmin, M.S. (eds) (2013) *Teaching Against Violence: Reassessing the Toolbox*. Budapest: ATGENDER & Central European University Press, pp. 31–60.

Nightingale, D.J. and Cromby, J. (2001) 'Critical Psychology and the Ideology of Individualism'. *Journal of Critical Psychology, Counselling and Psychotherapy*, 1 (2): 117–28.

Nolte, D. (1986) 'The Law Is Male and White: Meeting with the Black Author, Audre Lorde'. *In* Wylie Hall, J. (ed.) (2004) *Conversations with Audre Lorde*. Jackson, MS: University Press of Mississippi, pp. 143–5.

Oliver, K. (2001) *Witnessing: Beyond Recognition*. Minneapolis, MN: University of Minnesota Press.

Oliver, K. (2004) *The Colonization of Psychic Space: A Psychoanalytic Social Theory of Oppression*. Minneapolis, MN: University of Minnesota Press.

Parker, D. and Song, M. (eds) (2001) *Rethinking 'Mixed Race'*. London: Pluto Press.

Parker, I. (1999) 'Critical Psychology: Critical Links'. *Annual Review of Critical Psychology*, 1: 3–18.

Parker, I. (2005) *Qualitative Psychology: Introducing Radical Research*. Maidenhead: Open University Press.

Parker, I. (2007) *Revolution in Psychology: Alienation to Emancipation*. London: Pluto Press.

Parker, I. (2010) 'The Place of Transference in Psychosocial Research'. *Journal of Theoretical and Philosophical Psychology*, 30 (1): 17–31.

Parker, I. and Revelli, S. (eds) (2008) *Psychoanalytic Practice and State Regulation*. London: Karnac Books, Ltd.

Parker, I., Georgaca, E., Harper, D., McLaughlin, T. and Stowell-Smith, M. (eds) (1995) *Deconstructing Psychopathology*. London: Sage Publications, Ltd.

Parmar, P. and Kay, J. (1988) 'Frontiers'. *In* Wylie Hall, J. (ed.) (2004) *Conversations with Audre Lorde*. Jackson,MS: University Press of Mississippi, pp. 171–80.

Parton, N. (1999) 'Reconfiguring Child Welfare Practices: Risk, Advanced Liberalism and the Government of Freedom'. *In* Chambon, A., Irving, A. and Epstein, L. (1999) *Reading Foucault for Social Work*. New York: Columbia University Press, pp. 101–30.

Patel, P. and Siddiqui, H. (2010) 'Shrinking Secular Spaces: Asian Women at the Intersect of Race, Religion and Gender'. *In* Thiara, R.K. and Gill, A.K. (2010) *Violence Against Women in South Asian Communities: Issues for Policy and Practice*. London: Jessica Kingsley Publishers, pp. 102–27.

Pateman, C. and Mills, C. (2007) *Contract and Domination*. Cambridge: Polity Press.

Pellegrini, A. (1997) *Performance Anxieties: Staging Psychoanalysis, Staging Race*. New York: Routledge.

Pennycook, A. (1994) 'The Politics of Pronouns'. *ELT Journal*, 48 (2) April: 173–8.

Phoenix, A. and Pattynama, P. (eds) (2006) 'Special Issue on "Intersectionality"'. *European Journal of Women's Studies*, 13 (3) August: 187–92.

Prenowitz, E. (2008) 'Crossing Lines: Jacques Derrida and Hélène Cixous on the Phone'. *Discourse: Journal for Theoretical Studies in Media and Culture*, 30 (1 & 2) Winter & Spring: 123–56.

Probyn, E. (1993) *Sexing the Self: Gendered Positions in Cultural Studies.* London: Routledge.

Probyn, E. (2003) 'The Spatial Imperative of Subjectivity'. *In* Anderson, K., Domosh, M., Pile, S. and Thrift, N. (eds) (2003) *Handbook of Cultural Geography.* London: Sage Publications, Ltd., pp. 290–9.

Radhakrishnan, R. (2000) 'Postmodernism and the Rest of the World'. *In* Afzal-Khan, F. and Seshadri-Crooks, K. (eds) (2000) *The Pre-Occupation of Postcolonial Studies.* Durham, NC: Duke University Press, pp. 37–70.

Rape Crisis (England and Wales) (2004–2014) *Home Page.* [Online] [Accessed on 29th January, 2013] http://www.rapecrisis.org.uk/

Reuman, A.E. (1997) *In* Kulii, B.T., Reuman, A.E. and Trapasso, A. (1995 and 1997) *Audre Lorde's Life and Career.* Modern American Poetry. [Online] [Accessed on 29th January, 2013] http://www.english.illinois.edu/maps/poets/g_l/lorde/life.htm

Rich, A. (1979) 'An Interview with Audre Lorde'. *In* Wylie Hall, J. (ed.) (2004) *Conversations with Audre Lorde.* Jackson, MS: University Press of Mississippi, pp. 45–70.

Rose, N. (1985) *The Psychological Complex: Psychology, Politics and Society in England, 1869–1939.* London: Routledge and Kegan Paul.

Rose, N. (1998) *Inventing Our Selves: Psychology, Power, and Personhood.* Cambridge: Cambridge University Press.

Royle, N. (2003) *Jacques Derrida.* London: Routledge.

Royle, N. and Cixous, H. (2012) *Original Conversation between Prof. Nicholas Royle & Hélène Cixous on the University of Sussex Website.* [Online] [Accessed on 1st February, 2013] http://www.sussex.ac.uk/video/schools/english/HeleneCixousOnTheTelephone.mp3

Sánchez Calle, M.P. (1996) 'Audre Lorde's Zami and Black Women's Autobiography: Tradition and Innovation'. *BELLS: Barcelona English Language and Literature Studies*, 7: 161–9.

Savren, S. and Robinson, C. (1982) 'Interview: Audre Lorde Advocates Unity among Women'. *In* Wylie Hall, J. (ed.) (2004) *Conversations with Audre Lorde.* Jackson, MS: University Press of Mississippi, pp. 79–84.

Schiek, D. and Lawson, A. (eds) (2011) *European Union Non-Discrimination Law and Intersectionality: Investigating the Triangle of Racial, Gender and Disability Discrimination.* Farnham: Ashgate Publishing, Limited.

Searle, J. (1969) *Speech Acts: An Essay in the Philosophy of Language.* Cambridge: Cambridge University Press.

Searle, J. (1975) 'Indirect Speech Acts'. *In* Cole, P. and Morgan, J.L. (eds) (1975) *Syntax and Semantics. Volume 3: Speech Acts.* New York: Academic Press, pp. 59–82.

Seshadri-Crooks, K. (2000a) *Desiring Whiteness: A Lacanian Analysis of Race.* London: Routledge.

Seshadri-Crooks, K. (2000b) 'Surviving Theory: A Conversation with Homi K. Bhabha'. *In* Afzal-Khan, F. and Seshadri-Crooks, K. (eds) (2000) *The*

Pre-Occupation of Postcolonial Studies. Durham: Duke University Press, pp. 369–79.

Setti, N. (2012) 'Im/possible Voices'. *Darkmatter: In the Ruins of Imperial Culture,* May, 2012. [Peer-reviewed, open-access journal] [Online] [Accessed on 1st February, 2013] [No volume number, issue number or page numbers] http://www.darkmatter101.org/site/2012/05/18/impossible-voices/

Shildrick, M. and Price, J. (1998) *Vital Signs: Feminist Reconfigurations of the Bio/Logical Body.* Edinburgh: Edinburgh University Press.

Simmonds, F.N. (1996) 'Naming and Identity'. *In* Jarrett-Macavley, D. (ed.) (1996) *Reconstructing Womanhood, Reconstructing Feminism: Writings on Black Women.* London: Routledge, pp. 105–19.

Spelman, E.V. (1988a) 'Woman: The One and the Many'. *In* Kemp, S. and Squires, J. (eds) (1997) *Feminisms.* Oxford: Oxford University Press, pp. 235–6.

Spelman, E.V. (1988b) *Inessential Woman: Problems of Exclusion in Feminist Thought.* Boston: Beacon Press.

Spivak, G.C. (1979) 'Explanation and Culture: Marginalia'. *In* Landry, D. and MacLean, G. (eds) (1996) *The Spivak Reader: Selected Works of Gayatri Chakravorty Spivak.* New York: Routledge, pp. 29–51.

Spivak, G.C. (1980) 'Revolutions That as Yet Have No Model: Derrida's "Limited Inc."'. *In* Landry, D. and MacLean, G. (eds) (1996) *The Spivak Reader: Selected Works of Gayatri Chakravorty Spivak.* New York: Routledge, pp. 75–106.

Spivak, G.C. (1985) 'Feminism and Critical Theory'. *In* Landry, D. and MacLean, G. (eds) (1996) *The Spivak Reader: Selected Works of Gayatri Chakravorty Spivak.* New York: Routledge, pp. 53–74.

Spivak, G.C. (1986) 'Questions of Multi-culturalism'. *In* Spivak, G.C. (1990) *The Post-Colonial Critic: Interviews, Strategies, Dialogues* (ed. S. Harasym). New York: Routledge, pp. 59–66.

Spivak, G.C. (1988) 'Can the Subaltern Speak?' *In* Nelson, C. and Grossberg, L. (eds) (1988) *Marxism and the Interpretation of Culture.* Basingstoke: Macmillan, pp. 271–313.

Spivak, G.C. (1999) *A Critique of Postcolonial Reason: Toward a History of the Vanishing Present.* Cambridge, MA: Harvard University Press.

Spivak, G.C. (2006) *In Other Worlds: Essays in Cultural Politics.* London: Methuen.

Staples, R. (1979) 'The Myth of Black Macho: A Response to Angry Black Feminists'. *The Black Scholar,* 10 (8) March–April: 24–33.

Steiner, J. (1993) *Psychic Retreats: Pathological Organizations in Psychotic, Neurotic and Borderline Patients.* London: Routledge.

Suleri, S. (1992) 'Woman Skin Deep: Feminism and the Postcolonial Condition'. *In* Ashcroft, B., Griffiths, G. and Tiffin, H. (eds) (2006) *The Post-Colonial Studies Reader.* 2nd edn., London: Routledge, pp. 250–5.

Suture (1993) [Film] Directed by Scott McGehee and David Siegel. USA: MGM Home Entertainment.

Tate, C. (1982) 'Audre Lorde'. *In* Wylie Hall, J. (ed.) (2004) *Conversations with Audre Lorde.* Jackson, MS: University Press of Mississippi, pp. 85–100.

Taylor, Y., Hines, S. and Casey, M.E. (eds) (2010) *Theorizing Intersectionality and Sexuality.* Basingstoke: Palgrave Macmillan.

The Combahee River Collective (1977) 'A Black Feminist Statement'. *In* James, J. and Sharpley-Whiting, T.D. (eds) (2000) *The Black Feminist Reader*. Oxford: Blackwell Publishers Ltd., pp. 261–70.

Thieme, J. (2001) *Postcolonial Con-Texts: Writing Back to the Canon*. London: Continuum.

Thiongo, N.W. (1996) 'Borders and Bridges: Seeking Connections Between Things'. *In* Afzal-Khan, F. and Seshadri-Crooks, K. (eds) (2000) *The Pre-Occupation of Postcolonial Studies*. Durham, NC: Duke University Press, pp. 119–25.

Toll, R.C. (1974) *Blacking Up: The Minstrel Show in Nineteenth-Century America*. New York: Oxford University Press.

Truth, S. (1851) 'Ain't I a Woman?' *In* Collins, O. (ed.) (1998) *Speeches That Changed the World*. Louisville, KY: Westminster John Knox Press, pp. 208–9.

Unamuno, M.d. (2006) *Tragic Sense of Life* (trans. J.E. Crawford Flitch). New York: Barnes and Noble Publishing. [Originally published in 1913]

West, C. (1988) 'Marxist Theory and the Specificity of Afro-American Oppression'. *In* Nelson, C. and Grossberg, L. (eds) (1988) *Marxism and the Interpretation of Culture*. Basingstoke: Macmillan, pp. 17–34.

Westmoreland, M.W. (2008) 'Interruptions: Derrida and Hospitality'. *Kritike*, 2 (1) June: 1–10.

Whelehan, I. (1995) *Modern Feminist Thought: From the Second Wave to 'Post-Feminism'*. Edinburgh: Edinburgh University Press.

Wilkinson, S. and Kitzinger, C. (eds) (1996) *Representing the Other: A Feminism and Psychology Reader*. London: Sage Publications, Ltd.

Women's Resource Centre (2011) *Women-Only Services: Making the Case. A Guide for Women's Organisations*. [No publishing information listed]

Wylie Hall, J. (ed.) (2004) *Conversations with Audre Lorde*. Jackson, MS: University Press of Mississippi.

Yuval-Davis, N. (2006) 'Intersectionality and Feminist Politics'. *European Journal of Women's Studies*, 13 (3): 193–209.

Yuval-Davis, N. (2011) *The Politics of Belonging: Intersectional Contestations*. London: Sage Publications, Ltd.

Žižek, S. (2008a) *The Sublime Object of Ideology*. 2nd edn., London: Verso.

Žižek, S. (2008b) *In Defence of Lost Causes*. London: Verso.

Index